S0-ABA-355

IBM

International Technical Support Organization

DB2 9: pureXML
Overview and Fast Start
June 2006

SG24-7298

Note: Before using this information and the product it supports, read the information in "Notices" on page vii.

First Edition (June 2006)

This edition applies to Version 9.1 of IBM DB2 Universal Database.

© Copyright International Business Machines Corporation 2006. All rights reserved.
Note to U.S. Government Users Restricted Rights -- Use, duplication or disclosure restricted by GSA ADP Schedule Contract with IBM Corp.

Contents

© Copyright IBM Corp. 2006. All rights reserved.

Notices

This information was developed for products and services offered in the U.S.A.

IBM may not offer the products, services, or features discussed in this document in other countries. Consult your local IBM representative for information on the products and services currently available in your area. Any reference to an IBM product, program, or service is not intended to state or imply that only that IBM product, program, or service may be used. Any functionally equivalent product, program, or service that does not infringe any IBM intellectual property right may be used instead. However, it is the user's responsibility to evaluate and verify the operation of any non-IBM product, program, or service.

IBM may have patents or pending patent applications covering subject matter described in this document. The furnishing of this document does not give you any license to these patents. You can send license inquiries, in writing, to:
IBM Director of Licensing, IBM Corporation, North Castle Drive Armonk, NY 10504-1785 U.S.A.

The following paragraph does not apply to the United Kingdom or any other country where such provisions are inconsistent with local law: INTERNATIONAL BUSINESS MACHINES CORPORATION PROVIDES THIS PUBLICATION "AS IS" WITHOUT WARRANTY OF ANY KIND, EITHER EXPRESS OR IMPLIED, INCLUDING, BUT NOT LIMITED TO, THE IMPLIED WARRANTIES OF NON-INFRINGEMENT, MERCHANTABILITY OR FITNESS FOR A PARTICULAR PURPOSE. Some states do not allow disclaimer of express or implied warranties in certain transactions, therefore, this statement may not apply to you.

This information could include technical inaccuracies or typographical errors. Changes are periodically made to the information herein; these changes will be incorporated in new editions of the publication. IBM may make improvements and/or changes in the product(s) and/or the program(s) described in this publication at any time without notice.

Any references in this information to non-IBM Web sites are provided for convenience only and do not in any manner serve as an endorsement of those Web sites. The materials at those Web sites are not part of the materials for this IBM product and use of those Web sites is at your own risk.

IBM may use or distribute any of the information you supply in any way it believes appropriate without incurring any obligation to you.

Information concerning non-IBM products was obtained from the suppliers of those products, their published announcements or other publicly available sources. IBM has not tested those products and cannot confirm the accuracy of performance, compatibility or any other claims related to non-IBM products. Questions on the capabilities of non-IBM products should be addressed to the suppliers of those products.

This information contains examples of data and reports used in daily business operations. To illustrate them as completely as possible, the examples include the names of individuals, companies, brands, and products. All of these names are fictitious and any similarity to the names and addresses used by an actual business enterprise is entirely coincidental.

COPYRIGHT LICENSE:
This information contains sample application programs in source language, which illustrates programming techniques on various operating platforms. You may copy, modify, and distribute these sample programs in any form without payment to IBM, for the purposes of developing, using, marketing or distributing application programs conforming to the application programming interface for the operating platform for which the sample programs are written. These examples have not been thoroughly tested under all conditions. IBM, therefore, cannot guarantee or imply reliability, serviceability, or function of these programs. You may copy, modify, and distribute these sample programs in any form without payment to IBM for the purposes of developing, using, marketing, or distributing application programs conforming to IBM's application programming interfaces.

© Copyright IBM Corp. 2006. All rights reserved.

Trademarks

The following terms are trademarks of the International Business Machines Corporation in the United States, other countries, or both:

Celeron®	@server	Redbooks (logo)™
DB2 Universal Database™	IBM®	WebSphere®
DB2®	Itanium®	Xeon®
DB2 9®	pureXML™	
developerWorks®	Rational®	

The following terms are trademarks of other companies:

Java™ and all Java-based trademarks are trademarks of Sun Microsystems, Inc. in the United States, other countries, or both.

Microsoft™, Windows™, Windows NT™, and the Windows logo are trademarks of Microsoft Corporation in the United States, other countries, or both.

Intel®, Intel logo, Intel Inside®, Intel Inside logo, Intel Centrino™, Intel Centrino logo, Celeron®, Intel Xeon™, Intel SpeedStep®, Itanium®, and Pentium™ are trademarks or registered trademarks of Intel Corporation or its subsidiaries in the United States and other countries.

UNIX™ is a registered trademark of The Open Group in the United States and other countries.

Linux™ is a trademark of Linus Torvalds in the United States, other countries, or both.

Other company, product, or service names may be trademarks or service marks of others.

Foreword

Services Oriented Architectures (SOA) are an integral part of building an agile enterprise capable of making decisions quickly, and responding rapidly to new products and services opportunities, as well as to competitive threats. The explosive growth of XML data in businesses today across multiple industries has underscored the role of XML as the "fabric of Services Oriented Architectures" and the need to integrate XML data into enterprise information infrastructure.

DB2 9 (previously code-named "Viper") enables an information-centric approach to service oriented architecture implementations, which rely upon the ability to access a myriad of data stored across multiple formats. With its dual pure XML data management and traditional relational data capability, DB2 9 delivers information as a service in SOA environments, connecting information on-the-fly, where you need it, and when you need it!

XML data requires the same coveted qualities of service that relational databases provide: high availability, reliability, protection, and performance. The pureXML™ technology in DB2 9 unlocks the latent potential of XML by providing simple efficient access to XML with the same levels of security, integrity, and resiliency taken for granted with relational data. With pureXML innovation in DB2 9, your organization can expect breakthrough increases in availability, speed, and versatility of your XML information, along with dramatically reduced development and administrative costs.

This IBM Redbook serves as an introduction to the hybrid XML data services in DB2 9 for Linux, UNIX, and Windows. It also provides data server professionals a fast start for using and exploring pureXML capabilities in DB2 9 and get them started with leveraging XML information for maximum return.

SoC

Sal Vella
V.P., IBM DB2 Development

© Copyright IBM Corp. 2006. All rights reserved.

Preface

The new IBM DB2 9, (formerly codenamed "Viper"), features hybrid data management technology that incorporates proven relational capabilities with first-class support for storing, searching, sharing, validating, and managing XML data. The result is a reliable, scalable platform that provides high performance for accessing and integrating "traditional" corporate data as well as XML data.

Benefits of storing – or persisting – XML in a database management system vary according to the specific system in use. Potential benefits include:

► Improved employee productivity
► Improved IT resource utilization
► Reduced labor costs
► Quicker "time to value" for certain applications

You'll learn how this is possible as we explore different options for managing XML data and review the IBM solution.

This book is intended for IT managers, IT architects, DBAs, programmers, and other data server professionals.

This IBM Redbook is organized as follows:

► Chapter 1: Maximizing XML for maximum return. This chapter discusses the business case for XML technology in general and DB2 XML in particular. It includes case studies with quantified benefits, such as labor savings and code savings.

► Chapter 2: What's new in DB2 9: XML to the core. Technical overview of the release covering all major XML features.

► Chapter 3: Get off to a fast start with pureXML. First steps using DB2 9 XML, including database and table creation, inserting and importing data, and validating data. Java programming example provided in a side file.

► Chapter 4: Querying XML data with SQL. Tutorial about using SQL and SQL/XML to query XML data in DB2 9. Java programming example provided in a side file.

► Chapter 5: Querying XML data with XQuery. Tutorial about using XQuery to query XML data in DB2 9. Java programming example provided in a side file.

► Chapter 6: Developing Java applications for XML data. Tutorial on Java application development and the DB2 Developer Workbench.

► Chapter 7: Case study: Storebrand. Storebrand improves agility by integrating business processes with an IBM solution.

The team that produced this redbook

This redbook was produced by a team of IBM specialists at the IBM Silicon Valley Laboratory and Almaden Research Center, San Jose, CA, U.S., and at the IBM Toronto Lab, Toronto, Canada.

Cynthia M. Saracco is an IBM Senior Software Engineer, who works at IBM Silicon Valley Laboratory in the DB2 XML organization. She works on database management, XML, Web application development, and related topics.

Don Chamberlin is an IBM Fellow at Almaden Research Center. He is one of IBM's representatives in the W3C XML Query Working Group. He is also a co-author of the Quilt language proposal, which formed the basis for the XQuery design. Don is best known as co-inventor of the SQL database language and as author of two books on the DB2 database system. He holds a B.S. from Harvey Mudd College and a Ph.D. from Stanford University. He is also an ACM Fellow and a member of the National Academy of Engineering.

Rav Ahuja is a worldwide DB2 program manager based at the IBM Toronto Lab. He has been working with DB2 for Linux, UNIX, and Windows since version 1 and has held various roles in DB2 development, technical support, marketing, and product strategy. He works with customers and partners around the globe helping them build and benefit from DB2 and services-based solutions. Rav is a frequent contributor to DB2 papers, articles, and books. He holds a Computer Engineering degree from McGill University and MBA from University of Western Ontario.

Thanks to the following people for their contributions to this project:

Thore Thomassen
Storebrand Group

Seeling Cheung, Sarah Furr, Grant Hutchison, George Lapis, Nancy Miller, Matthias Nicola, Sriram Padmanabhan, Leslie Parham, Mackelly Ray, Gary Robinson, Hardeep Singh, Bert Van der Linden, and Susan Visser
IBM

Become a published author

Join us for a two- to six-week residency program! Help write an IBM Redbook dealing with specific products or solutions, while getting hands-on experience with leading-edge technologies. You'll team with IBM technical professionals, Business Partners and/or customers.

Your efforts will help increase product acceptance and customer satisfaction. As a bonus, you'll develop a network of contacts in IBM development labs, and increase your productivity and marketability.

Find out more about the residency program, browse the residency index, and apply online at:

ibm.com/redbooks/residencies.html

Comments welcome

Your comments are important to us!

We want our Redbooks to be as helpful as possible. Send us your comments about this or other Redbooks in one of the following ways:

► Use the online **Contact us** review redbook form found at:

ibm.com/redbooks

► Send your comments in an e-mail to:

redbook@us.ibm.com

► Mail your comments to:

IBM Corporation, International Technical Support Organization
Dept. HYTD Mail Station P099
2455 South Road
Poughkeepsie, NY 12601-5400

Notices

Chapters two through six in this IBM Redbook are based on articles that have been published in IBM developerWorks. They are updated and republished here with the permission of IBM developerWorks. Chapter one and chapter seven are IBM White Papers we have reprinted here.

Managing XML for maximum return

In an industry rife with acronyms, one three-letter combination makes many information technology leaders shudder: ROI (return on investment). Perhaps that's because ROI for any given project – or any given investment in supporting infrastructure – is usually difficult to quantify or predict. Yet few technology initiatives are funded without a convincing business case that describes the anticipated business value.[1]

This chapter explores the need for – and value of – managing XML data. It also reviews key technology alternatives and outlines which options may be most appropriate based on your business needs. But first, it addresses perhaps the most obvious question: why should you care?

---

[1] Information in this chapter was originally published as *Managing XML for Maximum Return*, by C. M. Saracco in an IBM White Paper, November 2005.

`ftp://ftp.software.ibm.com/software/data/pubs/papers/managingxml.pdf`

© Copyright IBM Corp. 2006. All rights reserved.

1.1 Why XML?

Since its debut in the 1990s, XML (eXtensible Markup Language) has emerged as a critical enabler to various technology initiatives. Service-oriented architectures (SOA), enterprise application integration (EAI), enterprise information integration (EII), Web services, and standardization efforts in many industries all rely on or make use of XML as an underlying technology.

Why? XML provides a neutral, flexible way of exchanging data among different devices, systems, and applications. Data is maintained in a self-describing format to accommodate a variety of ever-evolving business needs. Free software is available to help firms create, process, and transform XML data. All major industry vendors provide some level of XML support in their software offerings, and many have sought to exert considerable influence over XML-related standards - a sure sign of the technology's importance. Indeed, few industry analysts question the importance of XML today, and some are quite bullish on its prospects. ZapThink, for example, projects that the market for XML information exchange will approach nearly $3.8 billion by the end of the decade.

The business drivers behind XML's popularity are straightforward:

- ▶ A demand for increased business agility and efficiency
- ▶ A need to contain costs and "do more with less"
- ▶ A mandate to conform to regulatory requirements or comply with *de facto* industry standards

Let's look briefly at each of these in turn.

Building an agile business that can quickly respond to new market demands and competitive pressures implies that the underlying IT infrastructure must be easy to adapt and evolve. For example, tracking new information about customer preferences or buying behaviors cannot translate into a significant overhaul of a firm's production database; such an undertaking would be too time-consuming and costly. Similarly, firms cannot afford to have the success of a new business partnership or acquisition hampered by an inability to exchange information between different systems.

Cost containment implies a need to make maximum use of new and existing IT assets. It counters the notion of "rip-and-replace" inherent in some technology proposals. SOA enables firms to create building blocks – or services – for their IT assets, thereby promoting greater code reuse and a more adaptable infrastructure. XML is emerging as the preferred format for services to receive and publish data. It runs on a wide range of hardware devices, it's supported by proprietary and open source software, and it can accommodate a variety of data content.

Regulatory requirements and industry-specific initiatives are also driving the deployment of XML. As more business transactions are conducted through Web-based interfaces and electronic forms, government agencies and commercial enterprises bear greater responsibility for preserving the original order, request, claim, or submission. Doing so can be essential for legal reasons and good customer relations. Again, XML provides a straightforward means of capturing and maintaining the data associated with these electronic transactions; indeed, electronic forms are commonly based on XML. Furthermore, consortiums in many vertical industries and application-specific areas have already begun to define XML-based schemas to promote exchange of data. These include such diverse efforts as ACORD in the insurance industry, FpML and FIXML in the financial services industry, RosettaNet in supply chain management (SCM), XBRL for reporting in business reporting applications, and others.

Finally, many firms are revisiting their proprietary electronic data interchange (EDI) efforts in favor of XML-based solutions. Cost savings are part of the reason. According to one study published in *Computer Economics*, XML often supports business-to-business transactions more economically than EDI. Indeed, 88% of the surveyed XML users received a full return on their investments compared with only 65% of the EDI users. Furthermore, EDI solutions were more likely to exceed total cost of ownership (TCO) expectations than XML-based solutions. More than 40% of the EDI users suffered from higher-than-anticipated TCO, while only 17% of the XML users did so.

1.2 Managing XML: The need and benefits

All this is leading many organizations to search for a way to effectively manage their messages and documents written in XML. Often, their motivation is straightforward: as XML becomes more critical to the operations of an enterprise, it becomes an asset that needs to be shared, searched, secured, and maintained. Depending on its use, XML data may also need to be updated, audited, and integrated with other data. File systems aren't well-suited to supporting many of these tasks, particularly when scalability, concurrency, recovery, transaction management, and usability issues are taken into consideration. Database management software is a more appropriate choice, although until recently support for XML in many commercial offerings was somewhat limited.

Benefits of storing – or persisting – XML in a database management system vary according to the specific system in use. In a moment, we'll discuss several common architectural options and the trade-offs among them. However, potential benefits include:

► Improved employee productivity
► Improved IT resource utilization
► Reduced labor costs
► Quicker "time to value" for certain applications

You'll learn how this is possible as we explore different options for managing XML data and review the IBM solution.

1.3 Managing XML: The options

The growing use of XML hasn't been lost on database management systems (DBMS) vendors. Relational DBMS vendors began extending their products to accommodate "unstructured" and "semi-structured" data years ago, while other vendors built new, specialized DBMS products specifically to support XML. More recently, some relational DBMS vendors, such as IBM, moved to merge these two distinct efforts into one offering. The result is a multi-functional DBMS that works efficiently with data modeled in both tabular and hierarchical structures. Because XML files typically consist of nested hierarchies, the ability to effectively store, search, and update data in these hierarchies is significant.

Early attempts to support "non-traditional" forms of data often involved straightforward extensions to commercial relational DBMS products, and some of these extensions were ultimately applied to managing XML data. For example, character and binary large objects (CLOBs and BLOBs) are two data types commonly used to store the entire contents of an XML file as a single column in a row of a table. Furthermore, some vendors enable users to "shred" or decompose an XML document across multiple columns in one or more tables.

These early efforts to extend relational DBMS products to accommodate various forms of "non-traditional" data had merit and can be successfully used to address the needs of certain XML-based applications. However, each of these technologies introduced limitations that ultimately led some vendors to offer "native" support for XML data, which we'll discuss shortly.

1.3.1 Large objects and tables

Character or binary large objects (CLOBs or BLOBs) are one means of storing XML data in a tabular structure. By storing the XML document intact in a column of a row within a table, users don't need to break their document into pieces and map these pieces into various columns of one or more tables. Thus, the data modeling effort is simple and straightforward. Furthermore, complex joins aren't needed to reconstruct the original XML document because the document was never decomposed prior to storage.

However, using large objects – character or binary – has its drawbacks. Searching and retrieving a subset of the document can be expensive. New indexing technology may be needed to avoid the high cost of parsing XML for each query to determine which portions of the document satisfy the specified search criteria. Furthermore, updating large objects can be expensive. Often, client applications must provide the entire document to the DBMS for update, even if the client application only changed a small portion of it. This can result in unacceptably high processing costs, particularly if the XML document is very large.

1.3.2 Decomposition ("shredding") into tables

Performance problems for retrieving and updating portions of XML documents stored in large object columns led some vendors to offer document decomposition technology. This approach enables an administrator to map the elements and attributes of an XML document to columns in one or more tables. XML document values are then stored in these tables without their original tags.

"Shredding" XML data enables users to work with it in a purely tabular format, which implies several advantages. Users can leverage their existing SQL programming skills, as well as popular query and reporting tools, to work directly with selected portions of the "converted" XML data. This minimizes the need to develop new skills, which can translate into a higher level of productivity and even shorter application development cycles. Furthermore, runtime performance issues may be more predictable. No new indexing technology needs to be introduced, and updates against the converted XML data can be handled as efficiently as any other updates to data in standard SQL columns.

Unfortunately, the benefits of decomposing XML data often depend on the nature of the underlying XML document. This is because many XML documents contain heavily nested parent/child relationships and irregular structures. Shredding such documents may require a large number of tables, some of which may need to have values generated for foreign keys to capture the relationships inherent in the original XML documents. As an example, one firm with 1500 electronic forms needed more than 30,000 tables to contain their data.

Even in simpler cases, the contents of a single electronic form can seldom be normalized into a single table. Thus, mapping the XML data to a relational schema and managing the resulting environment can result in considerable labor for a database administrator. In some cases, it may not even be practical to shred an XML document, not only because of its internal complexity but because it may have many sparse attributes (information that's "missing" or irrelevant for a given record). Modeling such documents using a normalized relational data model is often too complex and expensive; however, de-normalizing the model may not be feasible because of built-in database limits for the maximum widths of rows or the maximum number of columns per table.

Moreover, querying a "shredded" document can require complex SQL statements that include many joins. Such statements are often difficult to develop and tune; this increases development costs, impedes "time to value," and ultimately causes runtime performance problems that impact the productivity of multiple users.

Furthermore, changes to the XML schema often break the mapping between the original XML schema and the relational database schema, resulting in added labor costs. For example, the introduction of multiple e-mail addresses for a single customer may require that a new table be created to comply with good database design principles (particularly normalization). However, introducing this new table implies implementing new primary/foreign key constraints, granting appropriate user access privileges, changing certain application logic, and so on. Such work can be substantial. Consider a relatively optimistic case in which a firm might need to update its 1000 electronic forms once or twice a year, and each form was mapped to a mere three tables. This would result in 3000 to 6000 schema changes that would have to be manually managed.

Finally, any inherent ordering of elements or any digital signatures associated with the original XML document are lost when the document is decomposed into columns spanning one or more tables. For some applications, preserving the original form of the XML document – along with any digital signature – is critical.

1.3.3 XML-only data management

Technical challenges associated with managing XML data in commercial relational DBMSs as large objects or through decomposition services prompted several firms to build XML-only database management products from scratch. By storing data in a hierarchical format and supporting a query language designed explicitly for XML data (XQuery), these products avoided many of the performance, schema management, and usability problems associated with other approaches.

However, this new breed of XML-only DBMS offerings failed to garner significant customer interest or support. Industry analysts estimate that the combined revenues of all XML-only DBMS products represent a tiny fraction of overall DBMS sales. Indeed, several early entrants into the XML DBMS field have gone out of business, shifted their focus, or been acquired by other firms.

The reasons why XML-only DBMS products have struggled vary. Many firms are reluctant to introduce a new, unproven DBMS environment into their IT infrastructures. Integration with existing relational DBMS products may be limited or non-existent, which poses a problem for the many firms that need a cohesive, enterprise-wide view of their critical data assets. Support for high levels of scalability, reliability, and availability are seldom robust in new DBMS products. Finally, few database administrators and application programmers have substantial skills in managing XML databases or querying collections of XML data using XQuery. Thus, introducing a new, unproven DBMS into an IT infrastructure can compromise its efficiency. Although skilled XML programmers may enjoy some productivity gains, high integration costs and system management challenges often mitigate overall benefits.

1.3.4 Hybrid data management

The growing use of XML and the lack of a comprehensive, efficient solution for managing this data along with other forms of corporate data have led to the development of hybrid database management software. Such software seeks to provide first-class support for both tabular and XML data structures, as well as SQL and XQuery. The objective of such systems is to preserve the benefits associated with commercial relational DBMS offerings – including high levels of scalability, reliability, availability, concurrency, and customer support – while making it easy to manage and integrate existing corporate data with data modeled in hierarchical XML structures.

Achieving this objective is best accomplished by building on a proven relational DBMS base and crafting new core capabilities within the system to efficiently index, search, and store XML data. Ideally, such a DBMS should optionally support validating XML data prior to storage and provide a simple means of coping with changing schemas.

For firms with existing relational DBMS environments, this approach enables them to derive new value from their investment. A hybrid DBMS enables users to seamlessly share, store, retrieve, and update both existing corporate data and XML data that had previously existed only in flat files or transient messages. Furthermore, it minimizes the amount of new skills required to incorporate XML data into their database environments, reducing labor costs and potentially speeding up project delivery cycles.

For firms concerned only with XML data management, the hybrid approach offers them a reliable and scalable infrastructure, the ability to leverage "relational" tools against their hierarchical XML data through the use of SQL/XML functions, the option of searching data in a query language designed for XML (XQuery), and the backing of major industry vendors. In addition, labor-intensive tasks such as mapping XML schemas to relational schemas and writing complex

SQL statements simply to query "converted" XML data are minimized or eliminated, which can improve both staff productivity and development cycle time.

1.4 Managing XML: The IBM solution

IBM's solution for managing XML data provides customers with a highly flexible, reliable, and efficient DBMS environment. Firms can use large objects or decomposition technology to model their XML data in tables, just as they've been able to do for years. However, DB2 9 (formerly codenamed "Viper") allows users to store, query, and process XML data in its hierarchical structure without sacrificing traditional DBMS support for transaction management, security, query optimization, and the like. We'll briefly review the first two options and then focus on the new capabilities in DB2's release 9 for managing XML data in its native format.

1.4.1 Relational extensions for XML

For years, DB2 customers have been able to use large objects, user-defined types, user-defined functions, and administrative tools to store XML data within tables. IBM continues to support these options and has even provided new capabilities in its DB2 9 release. Collectively, IBM's relational extensions for managing XML data with large objects or through XML decomposition and publishing technologies enable users to:

► Store XML data in a single column with minimal DBMS awareness of the internal structure of the XML data.

► Extract elements from an XML document and store their contents in multiple columns of one or more tables, in effect "converting" the XML data to tabular data. With DB2 9, new shredding technology supports larger XML documents and offers potential performance improvements.

► Store XML data type definitions (DTDs) for use in validating XML data.

► Compose and publish XML fragments from tables through the use of SQL/XML functions and mapping files. For example, users can write SQL queries that return results as well-formed XML.

► Invoke system-supplied stored procedures to administer their databases, generate XML documents, or "shred" XML documents into tables.

► Invoke system-supplied functions to insert XML documents, retrieve XML documents, extract element content or attribute values, and update XML documents.

These capabilities are most useful for situations in which users primarily want to perceive XML data as being part of a tabular data model that can be queried using SQL or SQL/XML functions. Applications that require high performance for searching and retrieving subsets of XML documents, that must cope with frequently changing XML schemas, or that require extensive use of XQuery and navigational expressions may be better served through new DB2 capabilities for native storage and management of XML data.

1.4.2 pureXML storage and management

DB2 9 features extensive new support for XML as a first-class data type. This "pure" support for XML includes new storage techniques for efficient management of hierarchical structures inherent in XML documents, new indexing technology to speed up retrieval of subsets of XML documents, new capabilities for validating XML data and managing changing XML schemas, new query language support (including native support for XQuery as well as new SQL/XML enhancements), new query optimization techniques, integration with popular application programming interfaces (APIs), and extensions to popular database utilities. The result is a single DBMS platform that offers the benefits of a commercial relational environment and a pureXML data environment.

Figure 1-1 illustrates the overall architecture of DB2 9. Both tabular and hierarchical storage models are supported through common engine components. Furthermore, client applications that need to work with both traditional SQL and XML data can use either SQL/XML or XQuery statements (or a combination of both). Full support for DB2 transaction semantics, security mechanisms, and distributed computing constructs (such as stored procedures) are supported for both SQL and XML data.

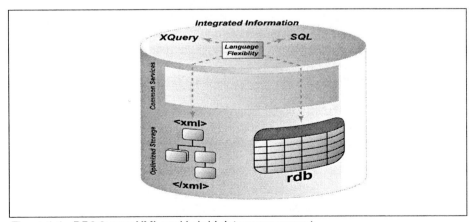

Figure 1-1   DB2 9: pureXML and hybrid data management

With DB2 9, collections of XML documents are captured in tables that contain one or more columns based on a new XML data type. This enables users to employ familiar SQL data definition language (DDL) statements to create database objects for storing their XML, although DB2 will treat the XML data differently internally. Specifically, it will automatically employ a custom storage management architecture that preserves the hierarchical structure of the original XML data and supports rapid retrieval of such data (or portions of it).

Tables created with XML data types may also contain columns with "traditional" SQL data types, including numeric data, character strings, date/time data, and others. Here's a simple example of how to define a table that maintains both types of data:

```
CREATE TABLE mytable (msgID INT PRIMARY KEY NOT NULL, msg XML)
```

After creating tables, users can issue INSERT statements or invoke the DB2 IMPORT facility to add data to their tables; such data may include both "traditional" SQL data types as well as DB2's new XML data type. Inserting or importing data in this manner makes it easy for customers to leverage their existing DB2 skills. However, these mechanisms hide the fact that DB2 manages the XML data in a way that's quite different from how it manages traditional SQL data types. In short, a parsed representation of each XML document is stored in its hierarchical format. If users instruct DB2 to validate their XML data prior to storage based on an XML schema, DB2 will annotate all nodes in the XML hierarchy with information about the schema types; otherwise, it will annotate the nodes with default type information. Furthermore, DB2 will automatically split portions of XML documents across multiple database pages as needed.

To help speed up searches, users can create indexes for specific elements or attributes of their XML documents. Such indexes are defined over XML patterns – essentially, XPath expressions without predicates – and can speed up the retrieval of queries targeting specific portions of XML documents. Full text search over XML documents is also supported, and specialized text indexes can be defined to improve performance of such searches.

Because DB2 9 is a "bilingual" product, users can search both XML data and traditional SQL data types with SQL or XQuery. Indeed, a single query can span XML and traditional SQL data stored within a single database. Furthermore, with WebSphere Information Integrator, firms can even write SQL-based queries that join and union XML data maintained in external files with data in DB2 and other non-IBM data sources. While details of supported query language capabilities are beyond the scope of this book, it's important to note that IBM's implementation is based on existing and rapidly emerging standards for both SQL and XQuery.

To efficiently process queries of XML data, DB2 leverages cost-based query optimization technology to evaluate different data access strategies and select a low-cost option. The large size of many XML documents, the complexity of query predicates found in many XPath expressions, and the need to preserve the order of elements contained within XML documents prompted IBM to develop new query operators and a new join algorithm specifically to speed up searches of XML data. The join algorithm provides for concurrent evaluation of "and" and "or" query predicates, as well as employs multiple cursors on XML indexes to locate the desired information quickly. Use of this new join technology is transparent to application programmers; DB2 will automatically evaluate queries and determine when it's beneficial to use it.

To serve a wide range of programmer needs, DB2 enables data stored in XML columns to be accessed through Java (JDBC), C (embedded SQL and call-level interface), COBOL (embedded SQL), PHP, and Microsoft's .NET environment (through the DB2.NET provider). To help administrators monitor and tune their databases, familiar facilities such as DB2 Snapshot, RUNSTATS, and EXPLAIN provide a "snapshot" of database activities at a given point-in-time, collect statistics about the nature of data within a database (including XML data), and report on the access path selected by the query optimizer (including new information about the use of indexes on XML data). Furthermore, DB2's built-in repository stores information relevant for validating XML data (including XML schemas and data type definitions) as well as other XML artifacts.

1.4.3 Early successes

Interest in DB2's new XML support has been strong, with firms in various industries evaluating an early release of the technology. Storebrand, one of Norway's largest providers of insurance and financial services, is among these firms. Storebrand Group was an early adopter of SOA and Web services, perceiving these technologies as important for helping the firm improve its customer focus and deliver greater value at a lower cost. According to Storebrand Senior Enterprise Architect Thore Thomassen, the firm considers XML to be an important integration mechanism. As such, XML data is an important asset that must be stored, managed, shared, and analyzed to support various business initiatives.

Thomassen noted that the firm's early experiments with the alpha release of DB2 9 were promising. Although Storebrand found each of DB2's three storage options – large objects, decomposition (or shredding), and use of native XML columns – to be useful, Thomassen discovered distinct advantages for native XML columns in certain comparative test situations. For example, preliminary work in test environments indicated that DB2's native XML data type could help them:

- Reduce the time it took to generate an internal report from more than one day to fewer than ten minutes.

- Cut the I/O portions of select Web services an average of 65% and decrease the maintenance time for these Web services by 20%.

- Implement a schema change (in response to new business requirements) in a few minutes instead of requiring a full day to prototype and test the change and a full week to deliver it.

- Minimize the labor required to program six new database search and retrieval scenarios. Using the native XML data type, a programmer completed the task in a ½ hour. By contrast, the same work required two hours with decomposition and eight hours with CLOBs.

In particular, Thomassen reviewed the results of one test project and noted, "Development time using the (DB2) XML native store is overall radically improved over shredding. Also, shredding often results in complex mappings, which mean that the developer needs deep competence in constructing SQL."

For more information regarding Storebrand benefits by using DB2 9, refer to Chapter 7, "Case study: Storebrand" on page 107.

Indeed, internal IBM studies have also demonstrated similar potential benefits. One comparative study published on IBM developerWorks involved a Web-based PHP application that used XML for capturing customer input and publishing data. Specifically, it explored the design and coding requirements for storing and searching the application's data using a traditional relational database environment (in which XML is shredded prior to storage) and DB2's native XML data type. Storing the XML data in its native format simplified the database schema considerably, resulting in only three tables of two columns each instead of four tables with up to nine columns each. Furthermore, certain aspects of the application, such as populating the database, were written with only one-third of the code. Finally, accommodating a new user requirement that resulted in an XML schema change was a more straightforward undertaking because administrators didn't need to change the underlying database schema and application programmers didn't need to rewrite the logic of their code.

For more information, refer to the article, "Use DB2 native XML with PHP", in IBM developerWorks by Hardeep Singh and Amir Malik, October 27, 2005, at:

`http://www-128.ibm.com/developerworks/db2/library/techarticle/dm-0511singh/`

1.5 Summary

XML messages and documents have emerged as key assets in many organizations, forcing IT executives and architects to find an effective means of managing this data for maximum advantage. Previous technology initiatives often fell short of achieving this goal. However, the new IBM DB2 9 release features hybrid data management technology that incorporates proven relational capabilities with first-class support for storing, searching, sharing, validating, and managing XML data. The result is a reliable, scalable platform that provides high performance for accessing and integrating "traditional" corporate data as well as XML data.

Early adopters are already noting the labor savings, shortened development cycles, and improved flexibility that DB2's XML support offers. In today's environment, such benefits can quickly translate into key competitive advantages.

2

What's new in DB2 9: XML to the core

The new DB2 9 release, (formerly codenamed "Viper"), features a significant architectural departure from prior versions. For the first time since its debut, DB2 Universal Database for Linux, UNIX, and Windows is providing a new query language, new storage technology, new indexing technology, and other features to support XML data and its inherent hierarchical structure. But don't worry, all of DB2's traditional database management features remain, including its support for SQL and tabular data structures. Explore DB2 9's new XML technology and learn why IBM now considers DB2 a "hybrid" or multi-structured database management system (DBMS).[1]

---

[1] Information in this chapter was originally published as "What's new in DB2 9: XML to the Core" by C. M. Saracco in IBM developerWorks, February 2006.

http://www-128.ibm.com/developerworks/db2/library/techarticle/dm-0602saracco/index.html

© Copyright IBM Corp. 2006. All rights reserved.

2.1 Introduction

Managing new forms of data often presents new challenges. Many IT leaders have discovered that's precisely the case when it comes to data in Extensible Markup Language (XML) format.

All too often, the obvious choices for managing and sharing XML data just don't cut it. File systems are fine for simple tasks, but they don't scale well when you need to cope with a large number of documents. Concurrency, recovery, security, and usability issues become unmanageable. Commercial relational database management systems (DBMSs) address those issues but fall short in other areas. They offer two fundamental database design options – storing each XML document intact as a single large object or "shredding" it into multiple columns often across multiple tables. In many situations, these options introduce performance problems, administrative challenges, increased query complexity, and other issues. Finally, XML-only DBMSs introduce a new, largely unproven environment into an IT infrastructure, raising concerns about integration, staff skills, and long-range viability.

The DB2 9 release of DB2 for Linux, Unix, and Windows platforms introduces another option. This new release supports XML data as a first-class type. To do so, IBM extended DB2 to include:

- ► New storage techniques for efficient management of hierarchical structures inherent in XML documents

- ► New indexing technology to speed up searches across and within XML documents

- ► New query language support (for XQuery), a new graphical query builder (for XQuery), and new query optimization techniques

- ► New support for validating XML data based on user-supplied schemas

- ► New administrative capabilities, including extensions to key database utilities

- ► Integration with popular application programming interfaces (APIs)

It's important to note that DB2's "native" support for XML, or pureXML, is *in addition* to its existing support for other technologies, including SQL, tabular data structures, and various DBMS features. As a result, users can create a single database object that manages both "traditional" SQL data and XML documents. Furthermore, they can write a single query that searches and integrates both forms of data.

This chapter explores these features as we delve into DB2's pureXML support. First, though, let's consider why proper management of XML data is important.

2.2 Potential benefits

With an increasing number of firms turning to XML to help them implement service-oriented architectures (SOA), exchange data among disparate systems and applications, and adapt to rapidly changing business conditions, many savvy IT leaders are looking for ways to effectively share, search, and manage the wealth of XML documents and messages that their firms are generating. DB2's new XML support is designed to help firms minimize the time and effort it takes to persist and use their XML data. This, in turn, can reduce development costs and improve business agility.

For example, the article, "Use DB2 native XML with PHP", in IBM developerWorks by Hardeep Singh and Amir Malik, October 27, 2005, at:

```
http://www-128.ibm.com/developerworks/db2/library/techarticle/dm-0511si
ngh/
```

illustrates how DB2's new XML support reduces the complexity of the database design and application code required to support an e-commerce Web site. Similarly, Chapter 1, "Managing XML for maximum return" on page 1, discusses early customer and IBM experiences involving comparative test scenarios that also indicate potential labor savings and improved cycle time.

What's behind these benefits? DB2 enables users to store XML documents intact with full DBMS knowledge of the document's internal structure. This eliminates or minimizes administrative and programming tasks associated with other alternatives. Furthermore, it can speed up searches across and within documents, and it enables customers to more readily accommodate changes to business requirements reflected in XML schemas.

2.3 Architectural overview

DB2 allows client applications to work with both tabular and XML data structures through the query language of their choice – SQL (including SQL with XML extensions, often referred to as "SQL/XML") or XQuery. As shown in Figure 2-1, engine-level components within DB2 support queries specified in either language.

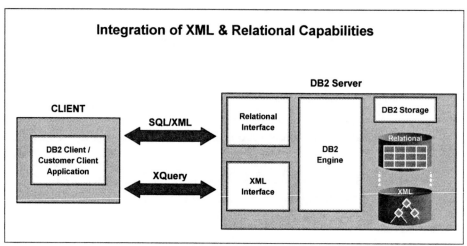

Figure 2-1   The architecture of the new DB2 9 release

To efficiently manage traditional SQL data types and XML data, DB2 includes two distinct storage mechanisms. We'll discuss the new XML storage technology shortly. However, it's important to note that the underlying storage mechanism used for a given data type is transparent to the application. In other words, the application doesn't need to explicitly specify which storage mechanism to use or manage physical aspects of storage, such as splitting portions of XML documents across multiple database pages. It simply enjoys the runtime performance benefits of storing and querying data in a format that's efficient for the target data.

Let's delve into the new DB2 XML features from a user's point of view.

2.4 Logical storage

Collections of XML documents are stored in DB2 tables containing one or more columns of the new XML data type. This enables administrators to use familiar SQL data definition language (DDL) statements to create database objects for persisting their XML data. However, this familiar interface masks the fact that DB2 stores the XML data differently, using new technology to preserve the XML data's hierarchical structure and support efficient searches spanning all or part of the original XML data.

To make it easy for users to integrate traditional forms of business data with XML data, DB2 administrators can create tables that contain columns of both traditional SQL data types and the new XML data type. Example 2-1 shows one such table.

Example 2-1   Creating a table with an XML column

```
create table items (
        id                 int       primary key not null,
        brandname          varchar(30),
        itemname           varchar(30),
        sku                int,
        srp                decimal(7,2),
        comments   xml
)
```

The first five columns of this table use traditional SQL data types to track information about each item for sale, including its ID number, brand name, item name, stock-keeping unit (SKU), and suggested retail price (SRP). A "comments" column contains XML data with feedback customers have shared regarding the item.

Note that the internal structure of the XML data isn't specified when creating a table with an XML column. This is by design. XML documents are self-describing, and their internal structure can vary considerably. DB2's only requirement for storing XML data is that it must be "well-formed", that is, it must adhere to certain syntax rules specified in the "W3C standard for XML". See "Resources" at the following Web site:

http://www-128.ibm.com/developerworks/db2/library/techarticle/dm-0602sa racco/index.html#resources

DB2's liberal approach provides users with considerable flexibility and makes it easy to store collections of XML documents that contain different attributes and internal structures due to evolving business requirements or situations where certain information is missing or irrelevant.

However, users who want to ensure that XML data conforms to their own structural rules can instruct DB2 to validate their data prior to storage. This is discussed in greater detail in 2.8, "XML schemas and validation" on page 25. Doing so essentially involves creating XML schemas (which are also part of the W3C XML standard) and registering these schemas with DB2. See "Resources" at the following Web site for more information on XML schemas:

http://www-128.ibm.com/developerworks/db2/library/techarticle/dm-0602sa racco/index.html#resources

At this point, you may be wondering how users populate a DB2 table with XML data. The answer is simple – they use one of two familiar DB2 mechanisms to do so. SQL INSERT statements as well as the DB2 IMPORT facility accommodate XML data in addition to other data types. (DB2 IMPORT issues INSERT statements behind the scenes.) If you're wondering why DB2 only supports data inserts through SQL and not XQuery, that answer is pretty simple, too – the first version of the emerging XQuery standard focuses on database read activities, not write activities. In the absence of a clearly accepted standard, IBM opted to offer its users two familiar means for persisting new XML data. See "Resources" at the following Web site for more information about the XQuery standard:

```
http://www-128.ibm.com/developerworks/db2/library/techarticle/dm-0602sa
racco/index.html#resources
```

2.5 Physical storage

As a practical matter, most users won't need to concern themselves with DB2's new physical storage management architecture for XML data. However, to help you understand what DB2 is doing behind the scenes, let's briefly discuss its internal approach to storing XML data.

DB2 stores and manipulates XML data in a parsed format that reflects the hierarchical nature of the original XML document. As such, it uses trees and nodes as its model for storing and processing XML data. If users instruct DB2 to validate their XML data against a registered XML schema prior to storage, DB2 will annotate all nodes in the XML hierarchy with information about the schema types; otherwise, it will annotate the nodes with default type information.

Given the earlier definition of an "items" table, let's review a sample XML document to be stored in that table. As shown in Figure 2-2, this XML document contains multiple elements represented in a hierarchy, including a root "Comments" element and one or more individual "Comment" elements pertaining to a given item. Associated with each comment is a comment identifier, customer information that may include sub-elements for the customer's name and e-mail address, the text of the customer's message or comment, and an indicator of whether or not the customer would like a reply.

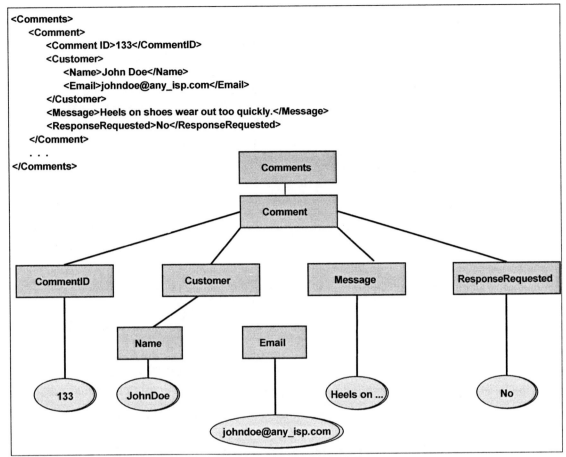

```
<Comments>
    <Comment>
        <Comment ID>133</CommentID>
        <Customer>
            <Name>John Doe</Name>
            <Email>johndoe@any_isp.com</Email>
        </Customer>
        <Message>Heels on shoes wear out too quickly.</Message>
        <ResponseRequested>No</ResponseRequested>
    </Comment>
    . . .
</Comments>
```

Figure 2-2   Sample XML document and its hierarchical representation

Upon storage, DB2 will preserve the internal structure of this document, converting its tag names and other information into integer values. Doing so helps conserve disk space and also improves the performance of queries that use navigational expressions. For example, DB2 might convert the "Comments" tag in Figure 2-2 to a "0" upon storage. However, users aren't aware of this internal representation.

Finally, DB2 will automatically split portions of a document – that is, nodes of the document tree – across multiple database pages as needed. Indeed, DB2 can split a collection (or sub-tree) of nodes at any level of the document hierarchy as needed. In such cases, DB2 automatically generates and maintains a "regions" index to provide an efficient means of tracking the physical representation of the entire document.

2.6 Indexing

Along with new hierarchical storage management support for XML, DB2 features new indexing technology to speed up searches involving XML data. Like their relational counterparts, these new XML indexes are created with a familiar SQL DDL statement: CREATE INDEX. However, in addition to specifying the target column to index, users also specify an "xmlpattern" – essentially, an XPath expression without predicates – to identify the subset of the XML document of interest.

For example, using the earlier "items" table definition and the corresponding sample XML document shown in Example 2-2, an administrator might issue the following statement to index all comment identifiers ("CommentID" values) contained in the "comments" column. Recall that the "CommentID" element in our sample document is a child of the "Comment" element, which itself is a child of the root "Comments" element.

Example 2-2 Creating an index for an XML column

```
create index myindex on items(comments) generate key
using xmlpattern '/Comments/Comment/CommentID' as sql double
```

A few details are worth noting. The path specified in the "xmlpattern" clause is case specific. Thus, "/Comments/Comment/CommentID" will not index the same XML element values as "/comments/comment/commentid." Furthermore, because DB2 doesn't require a single XML schema for a given XML column, DB2 may not know what data type to associate with the specified pattern. Users must specify the data type explicitly using one of the supported SQL types (VARCHAR, VARCHAR HASHED, DOUBLE, DATE, and TIMESTAMP).

Finally, although an SQL DDL statement is used to create an XML index, an index over XML data isn't the same as an index over columns of traditional SQL data types. While details of DB2's XML indexing technology are beyond the scope of this chapter, you may have noticed two significant differences:

- ► Indexes on XML data typically involve only a subset of the document's (column's) contents. By contrast, indexes on traditional SQL data always involve the entire column's content.

- ► A single row in a table may result in multiple XML index entries because a single XML document may contain zero, one, or many "nodes" that match the specified xmlpattern. By contrast, a non-XML index contains one entry for each row in the table.

For certain applications, full-text search can be critical. IBM has extended DB2's previous text search capabilities to include data stored in XML columns.

Extensions to the CREATE INDEX statement enable administrators to create full text indexes to help improve the performance of such searches.

2.7 Query language and optimization

DB2's new XML support includes new query language capabilities. Programmers can now search for data using SQL or XQuery, a new query language that supports navigational (or path-based) expressions. Indeed, applications can freely employ statements from both query languages, and a single query statement can actually incorporate both SQL and XQuery.

We don't have time to explore the breadth and depth of these capabilities in this chapter, so let's just discuss a few highlights. If you're an SQL programmer with no prior XML experience, you'll be relieved to learn that a simple SQL statement will enable you to retrieve the contents of data stored in XML columns. For example, these two familiar queries will return all the data in the "items" table related to a specific stock-keeping unit (SKU), including XML documents with customer comments. See Example 2-3.

Example 2-3   Querying XML data with SQL

```
select * from items where sku = 112233

select id, brandname, itemname, sku, srp, comments from items
    where sku = 112233
```

Now let's consider a slightly different situation, in which you want to retrieve only the messages contained within customer comments of the "items" table, and you want to do so using XQuery. Here's perhaps the simplest way to formulate the statement. See Example 2-4.

Example 2-4   Querying XML data with XQuery

```
xquery db2-fn:xmlcolumn('ITEMS.COMMENTS')/Comments/Comment/Message
```

Because DB2 supports two query languages, users must prefix XQuery statements with the keyword "xquery." The "db2-fn:xmlcolumn" function is one way to specify the target data to be queried. It requires a parameter specifying the XML column of the desired table: in this case, the COMMENTS column of the ITEMS table. You've further restricted your target data to a specific subset of XML data: namely, values of the "Message" element, which is a child of the "Comment" element, which itself is a child of the root "Comments" element. (See Figure 2-2 on page 21).

The same query can be formulated using FLWOR expressions commonly associated with XQueries. FLWOR expressions – an informal way of referring to **for, let, where, order by**, and **return** clauses – enable programmers to iterate over groups of nodes within XML documents and to bind variables to intermediate results. For this sample query, you can use **for** and **return** expressions to retrieve messages from customer comments, as shown in Example 2-5.

Example 2-5   Using FOR and RETURN clauses of XQuery

```
xquery for $y in db2-fn:xmlcolumn('ITEMS.COMMENTS')/Comments/Comment
return ($y/Message)
```

It's worth noting that DB2 9 ships with a Developer Workbench, an Eclipse-based development tool that includes a graphical XQuery builder to help users generate and test queries.

Both SQL and XQuery can be combined in a single statement to restrict searches for both XML and non-XML columns. For example, consider the following XQuery statement (Example 2-6).

Example 2-6   Combining SQL and XQuery in one statement

```
xquery db2-fn:sqlquery('select comments from items
where srp > 100')/Comments/Comment/Message
```

The db2-fn:sqlquery clause restricts the input to the broader XQuery statement; specifically, only customer comments associated with items carrying a suggested retail price (srp) of more than $100 are passed as input. Further XQuery information indicates that DB2 should only return the "Message" portions of such comments.

A number of papers and Web sites can help you get up to speed on DB2's SQL/XML extensions, DB2's support for XQuery, and the emerging XQuery standard. See "Resources" at the following Web site for pointers:

```
http://www-128.ibm.com/developerworks/db2/library/techarticle/dm-0602sa
racco/index.html#resources
```

Finally, this discussion of query languages may leave you wondering about a related topic: query optimization. DB2 has two query language parsers: One for XQuery and one for SQL. Both generate a common, language-neutral, internal representation of queries. This means that queries written in either language are afforded the full benefits of DB2's cost-based query optimization techniques, which include efficient rewriting of query operators and selection of a low-cost data access plan. In addition, DB2 can leverage new query and join operators, as well as new index processing techniques, to provide strong runtime performance for queries involving XML documents.

2.8 XML schemas and validation

The flexible nature of XML sometimes concerns database professionals who worry about data quality. As we've already noted, DB2 enables users to store any well-formed XML document in any column defined on the new XML data type. Thus, a single column can contain documents with different structures (or schemas) as well as different content. When the nature of the data to be captured is unclear or difficult to predict, such flexibility can be an absolute necessity. But in other cases, it can be a liability. That's why DB2 gives users the option of registering their XML schemas and instructing DB2 to validate XML documents against these schemas prior to storage.

If you're not familiar with XML schemas, they're simply well-formed XML documents that dictate the structure and content of other documents. For example, XML schemas specify which elements are valid, in what order these elements should appear in a document, which XML data types are associated with each element, and so on. Various tools can help you create XML schemas from existing XML documents, including IBM WebSphere Studio line and its follow-on brand of Rational products.

Users can elect to store different XML documents that correspond to different registered schemas within a single column. This is significant because evolving business needs can impact the structure and content of XML data that needs to be captured. Considering our earlier "items" table, imagine that several months after this table was deployed you decided to capture additional information in the XML column, such as more customer contact information, a record of the actions taken in response to certain comments, and so on. DB2 can accommodate these new enhancements without forcing users to change the table's structure or any applications that rely on it. Indeed, existing data (based on an "old" XML schema) can remain in place, and new data can be added that complies with one or more new schemas. In this way, administrators can support new business requirements with minimal deployment time and cost. Furthermore, they don't need to compromise the integrity of their XML to do so - they can simply supply DB2 with new information about what's "valid" for their XML data.

Registering an XML schema in DB2's internal repository is simple. DB2 provides stored procedures to automate the process, or administrators can manually issue corresponding commands. A single schema can be used to validate multiple XML columns in multiple tables, if desired.

2.9 Administrative support

DB2's new support for XML includes extensions to familiar tools and utilities to help administrators manage and tune their databases. For example, backup and restore facilities – including high availability data replication for failover situations – all support documents stored in XML columns. Similarly, extensions to the IMPORT and EXPORT facilities now operate on both traditional SQL and XML data. Thus, you could issue a single IMPORT command to populate the entire "items" table (reading XML data from native files) and issue a single EXPORT command to write all the table's data to external files.

In addition, DB2's graphical administrative tool, the DB2 Control Center, enables administrators to browse tables containing XML data, create and manage XML-based indexes, issue SQL/XML and XQuery statements, and perform a number of other administrative tasks. Since performance is often a key concern, appropriate DB2 facilities have also been extended to accommodate XML data. These include the DB2 Snapshot Monitor, which provides a point-in-time summary or "snapshot" of DB2 activities; RUNSTATS, which collects statistics about the nature of the data stored in a DB2 database; and EXPLAIN, which reports on which access path the query optimizer selected to satisfy a given request. Examining EXPLAIN output can enable an administrator to determine which XML indexes are being used.

2.10 Programming language extensions

DB2's new XML support wouldn't be very useful if the XML stored in its databases wasn't readily accessible to programmers. Recognizing this, IBM implemented enhancements to its various programming language interfaces to support easy access to its XML data. These enhancements span Java (JDBC), C (embedded SQL and call-level interface), COBOL (embedded SQL), PHP, and Microsoft's .NET environment (through the DB2.NET provider).

Because the application programming interface (API) varies according to the programming language in use, we won't be reviewing each of these extensions here. However, you can read a summary of these extensions in a recently published conference paper *Native XML Support in DB2 Universal Database*, see "Resources" at the following Web site:

```
http://www-128.ibm.com/developerworks/db2/library/techarticle/dm-0602sa
racco/index.html#resources
```

Or refer to the article, "Use DB2 native XML with PHP", in IBM developerWorks by Hardeep Singh and Amir Malik, October 27, 2005, at:

http://www-128.ibm.com/developerworks/db2/library/techarticle/dm-0511si
ngh/

2.11 Summary

The DB2 9 release is the first IBM implementation of a "hybrid" or multi-structured database management system. In addition to supporting a tabular data model, DB2 also supports the native hierarchical data model found in XML documents and messages. Users can freely mix and match storage of traditional SQL data and XML in a single table. They can also query and integrate both forms of data using SQL (with XML extensions, if desired) and XQuery, the emerging standard for querying XML data. By building on a proven database management infrastructure, IBM is providing DB2 9 users with sophisticated support for both relational and pureXML DBMS technologies.

3

Get off to a fast start with pureXML

In this chapter, learn how to create database objects for managing your XML data and how to populate your DB2 database with XML data.[1]

DB2's new release 9, (formerly codenamed "Viper"), is the first database management system to support both tabular (SQL-based) and hierarchical (XML-based) data structures in their native format. If you're curious about DB2's new "native" support for XML and want to get off to a fast start, you've come to the right place. We walk through several common tasks, such as:

► Creating database objects for managing XML data, including a test database, sample tables, and views

► Populating the database with XML data using INSERT and IMPORT statements

► Validating your XML data. Develop and register your XML schemas with DB2, and use the XMLVALIDATE option when importing data.

---

[1] Information in this chapter was originally published as "Get off to a fast start with XML in DB2 9", by C. M. Saracco in IBM developerWorks, March 2006.

```
http://www-128.ibm.com/developerworks/db2/library/techarticle/dm-0603sa
racco/
```

© Copyright IBM Corp. 2006. All rights reserved.

3.1 Creating database objects

To get started, let's create a single DB2 Unicode database. In DB2 9, only Unicode databases can store both XML documents and more traditional forms of SQL data, such as integer, date/time, varying length character strings, and so on. Later, you'll create objects within this database to manage both XML and other types of data.

3.1.1 Creating a test database

To create a new DB2 Unicode "test" database, open a DB2 command window and issue a statement specifying a Unicode codeset and a supported territory, as shown in Example 3-1.

Example 3-1   Creating a database for storing XML data

```
create database test using codeset UTF-8 territory us
```

Once you create a Unicode database, you don't need to issue any special commands or take any further action to enable DB2 to store XML data in its native hierarchical format. Your DB2 system is ready to go.

3.1.2 Creating sample tables

To store XML data, create tables that contain one or more XML columns. These tables serve as logical containers for collections of documents; behind the scenes, DB2 actually uses a different storage scheme for XML and non-XML data. However, using tables as a logical object for managing all forms of supported data simplifies administration and application development issues, particularly when different forms of data need to be integrated in a single query.

You can define DB2 tables to contain only XML columns, only columns of traditional SQL types, or a combination of both. This chapter models the latter. Example 3-2 connects to the "test" database and creates two tables. The first is an "items" table that tracks information about items for sale and comments that customers have made about them. The second table tracks information about "clients," including contact data. Note that "comments" and "contactinfo" are based on the new DB2 XML data type, while all other columns in the tables are based on traditional SQL data types.

Example 3-2   Creating tables for XML data

```
connect to test;
```

```
create table items (
  id          int primary key not null,
  brandname   varchar(30),
  itemname    varchar(30),
  sku         int,
  srp         decimal(7,2),
  comments    xml
);

create table clients(
  id          int primary key not null,
  name        varchar(50),
  status      varchar(10),
  contactinfo xml
);
```

If you look closely at these table definition examples, you'll notice that neither specified the internal structure of the XML documents to be stored in the "comments" or "contactinfo" columns. This is an important DB2 feature. Users don't need to pre-define an XML data structure (or, more accurately, an XML schema) in order to store their data. Indeed, DB2 can store any well-formed XML document in a single column, meaning that XML documents based on different schemas – or documents not associated with any registered schema – can be stored within the same DB2 column. This chapter discusses this feature further when we explore how to store data in DB2.

3.1.3 Creating views

Optionally, you can create views over tables containing XML data, just as you can create views over tables containing only traditional SQL data types. Example 3-3 creates a view of clients with a "Gold" status.

Example 3-3   Creating a view that contains XML data

```
create view goldview as
select id, name, contactinfo
from clients where status='Gold';
```

3.1.4 A note about indexes

Finally, it's worth noting that you can create specialized indexes on your XML columns to speed up searches of your data. Because this is an introductory chapter and the sample data is small, this chapter will not cover that topic. However, in production environments, defining appropriate indexes can be critical to achieving optimal performance. See "Resources," at the following Web site, for help on how to learn more about DB2's new indexing technology:

```
http://www-128.ibm.com/developerworks/db2/library/techarticle/dm-0603sa
racco/
```

3.2 Storing XML data

With your tables created, you can now populate them with data. You can do so by issuing SQL INSERT statements directly or by invoking the DB2 IMPORT facility, which issues INSERT statements behind the scenes.

3.2.1 Using INSERT statements

With INSERT, you supply DB2 with the raw XML data directly. That's perhaps easiest to do if you've written an application and stored the XML data in a variable. But if you're just getting started with DB2 9 and don't want to write an application, you can issue your INSERT statements interactively. (Many people find it convenient to use the DB2 Command Editor, although you can also use the command line processor, if you'd prefer.)

To use the DB2 Command Editor, launch the DB2 Control Center. From the "Tools" pull-down menu at the top, select the Command Editor. A separate window will appear, which should look like Figure 3-1.

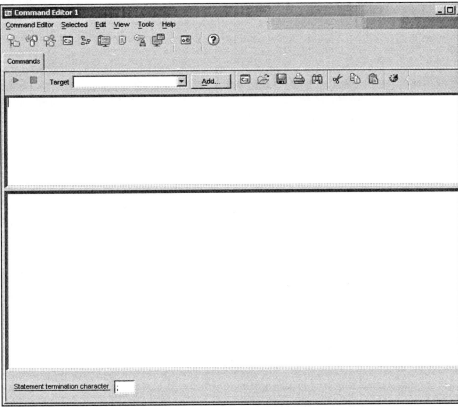

Figure 3-1   DB2 Command Editor

Type the following statements (see Example 3-4) into the upper pane.

Example 3-4   Inserting XML data interactively

```
connect to test;

insert into clients values (77, 'John Smith', 'Gold',
    '<addr>111 Main St., Dallas, TX, 00112</addr>')
```

Click the green arrow at left to execute the command.

In this case, the input document was quite simple. If the document was large or complex, it would be impractical to type the XML data into the INSERT statement as shown. In most cases, you'd write an application to insert the data using a host variable or a parameter marker. For a brief Java coding example, refer to the following Web site:

```
http://www-128.ibm.com/developerworks/db2/library/techarticle/dm-0603sa
racco/sidefile1.html
```

However, since this is an introductory tutorial, we won't be discussing application development topics in detail. Instead, we'll discuss another option for populating DB2 XML columns with data – using the IMPORT facility.

3.2.2 Using DB2 IMPORT

If you already have your XML data in files, the DB2 IMPORT facility provides a simple way for you to populate your DB2 tables with this data. You don't need to write an application. You just need to create a delimited ASCII file containing the data you want to load into your table. For XML data stored in files, a parameter specifies the appropriate file names.

You can create the delimited ASCII file using the text editor of your choice. (By convention, such files are usually of type .del.) Each line in your file represents a row of data to be imported into your table. If your line contains an XML Data Specifier (XDS), IMPORT will read the data contained in the referenced XML file and import that into DB2. For example, the first line in Figure 3-2 contains information for Ella Kimpton, including her ID, name, and customer status. Her contact information is included in the Client3227.xml file.

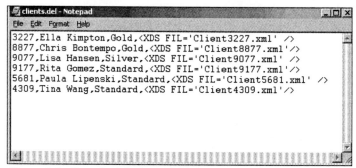

Figure 3-2 Sample delimited ASCII file for input to DB2 IMPORT

The content of the Client3227.xml file is shown in Figure 3-3. As you can see, the file contains XML elements for Ella Kimpton's address, phone numbers, fax number, and e-mail.

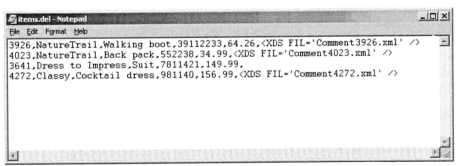

```
Client3227.xml - Notepad                                    _|□|×|
File  Edit  Format  Help
<?xml version="1.0"?>
<Client
xmlns:xsi="http://www.w3.org/2001/XMLSchema-instance"
xsi:noNamespaceSchemaLocation="http://bogus">
        <Address>
                <street>5401 Julio Ave.</street>
                <city>San Jose</city>
                <state>CA</state>
                <zip>95116</zip>
        </Address>
        <phone>
                <work>4084630000</work>
                <home>4081111111</home>
                <cell>4082222222</cell>
        </phone>
        <fax>4087776666</fax>
        <email>love2shop@yahoo.com</email>
</Client>
```

Figure 3-3   Sample client XML file

Perhaps you're curious about importing data if you don't have XML files for all the rows you wish to insert. That's easy to do. Omit the XDS information from your input file. For example, the items.del file in Figure 3-4 omits the name of an XML file for Item 3641 (the "Dress to Impress" suit). As a result, the XML column for this row will not contain any data.

```
items.del - Notepad                                         _|□|×|
File  Edit  Format  Help
3926,NatureTrail,Walking boot,39112233,64.26,<XDS FIL='Comment3926.xml' />
4023,NatureTrail,Back pack,552238,34.99,<XDS FIL='Comment4023.xml' />
3641,Dress to Impress,Suit,7811421,149.99,
4272,Classy,Cocktail dress,981140,156.99,<XDS FIL='Comment4272.xml' />
```

Figure 3-4   Sample delimited ASCII file with no XML Data Specifier for one row

With your XML files and delimited ASCII files available, you're now ready to use DB2 IMPORT. The following statement in Example 3-5 will import the contents specified in the clients.del file in the C:/XMLFILES directory into the "clients" table.

Example 3-5   Importing data into the "clients" table

```
import from clients.del of del xml from C:/XMLFILES insert into
user1.clients;
```

The clients.del file shown in Figure 3-2 on page 34 contains data for six rows, including references to six XML files. Successfully executing an IMPORT command will result in output similar to Figure 3-5.

```
DB2 CLP                                                              _ |□| x|
import from clients.del of del xml from C:/XMLFIles insert into saracco.clients
SQL3109N  The utility is beginning to load data from file "clients.del".

SQL3110N  The utility has completed processing.  "6" rows were read from the
input file.

SQL3221W  ...Begin COMMIT WORK. Input Record Count = "6".

SQL3222W  ...COMMIT of any database changes was successful.

SQL3149N  "6" rows were processed from the input file.  "6" rows were
successfully inserted into the table.  "0" rows were rejected.


Number of rows read       = 6
Number of rows skipped    = 0
Number of rows inserted   = 6
Number of rows updated    = 0
Number of rows rejected   = 0
Number of rows committed  = 6


C:\XMLfiles>_
```

Figure 3-5   Sample output of DB2 IMPORT

Independent software vendors, such as Exegenix, offer tools that can help you convert Word, PDF, and other document formats into XML for import into DB2.

3.3 Validating your XML data

The INSERT and IMPORT examples just discussed will write any well-formed XML data to your tables. They don't validate that data – that is, they don't verify that the data conforms to a particular XML schema and therefore adheres to a certain structure. It's possible to direct DB2 to do that, however. Let's explore one way to do so.

3.3.1 Step 1: Creating an XML schema

To validate XML data, you need to define an XML schema that specifies acceptable XML elements, their order and data types, and so on. XML schemas are a W3C industry standard and are written in XML. While it's beyond the scope of this paper to explain the features of XML schemas, various tutorials are available on the Web. See "Resources" at the following Web site:

http://www-128.ibm.com/developerworks/db2/library/techarticle/dm-0603sa racco/

There are many ways to develop XML schemas, ranging from using your favorite text editor to manually create your schema to using tools to graphically design or generate a schema. Independent software vendors, such as MDXSYS Limited, provide such XML tools, and IBM also offers XML schema generation support through its Java-integrated development environment.

For example, with IBM WebSphere Studio, you can import the Client3227.xml file, shown in Figure 3-3, into a Web project. Right-click, using your mouse, and elect to **Generate** → **XML Schema**. This will generate a valid XML schema for your particular input file, as shown in Figure 3-6. You can then modify the file (if necessary) and register it with DB2.

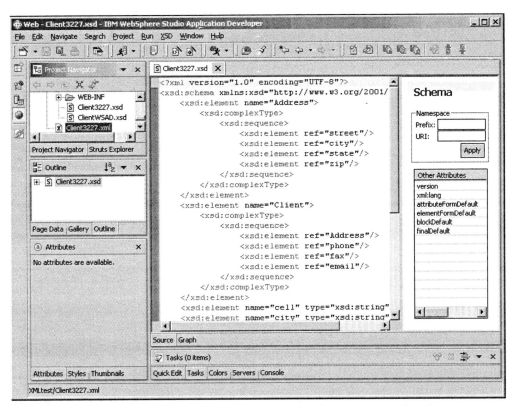

Figure 3-6   Using WebSphere Studio to generate an XML schema from an XML file

Let's assume you need to make your XML schema rather flexible so that you can collect different types of contact information for different customers. For example, some customers may provide you with multiple phone numbers or e-mail addresses, while others may not do so.

The XML schema shown in Figure 3-7, which was derived from the schema generated by WebSphere Studio, allows for this flexibility. It includes additional specifications about the minimum and maximum number of occurrences ("minOccurs" and "maxOccurs") allowed for a given element. In this case, the customer isn't required to give you any of the contact information you'd like to collect. However, if a customer chooses to give you e-mail information, this schema will enable conforming documents to contain up to five e-mail addresses (that is, five "email" element values).

File   Edit   View   Insert   Format   Help

```
<?xml version="1.0" encoding="UTF-8"?>
<xsd:schema xmlns:xsd="http://www.w3.org/2001/XMLSchema">
    <xsd:element name="Address">
        <xsd:complexType>
            <xsd:sequence>
                <xsd:element ref="street" minOccurs="0"/>
                <xsd:element ref="apt" minOccurs="0"/>
                <xsd:element ref="city" minOccurs="0"/>
                <xsd:element ref="state" minOccurs="0"/>
                <xsd:element ref="zip" minOccurs="0"/>
            </xsd:sequence>
        </xsd:complexType>
    </xsd:element>
    <xsd:element name="Client">
        <xsd:complexType>
            <xsd:sequence>
                <xsd:element ref="Address" minOccurs="0" maxOccurs="5"/>
                <xsd:element ref="phone" minOccurs="0" maxOccurs="1"/>
                <xsd:element ref="fax" minOccurs="0" maxOccurs="1"/>
                <xsd:element ref="email" minOccurs="0" maxOccurs="5"/>
            </xsd:sequence>
        </xsd:complexType>
    </xsd:element>
    <xsd:element name="cell" type="xsd:string"/>
    <xsd:element name="city" type="xsd:string"/>
    <xsd:element name="email" type="xsd:string"/>
    <xsd:element name="fax" type="xsd:string"/>
    <xsd:element name="home" type="xsd:string"/>
    <xsd:element name="phone">
        <xsd:complexType>
            <xsd:sequence>
                <xsd:element ref="work" minOccurs="0"/>
                <xsd:element ref="home" minOccurs="0"/>
                <xsd:element ref="cell" minOccurs="0"/>
            </xsd:sequence>
        </xsd:complexType>
    </xsd:element>
    . . .
</xsd:schema>
```

For Help, press F1

Figure 3-7   Sample XML schema for client contact information

As you may have noted, XML schemas also contain type information. While the schema shown in Figure 3-7 simply specifies that all base elements are to be treated as strings, most production XML schemas make use of other data types as well, such as integer, decimal, date, and so on. If you validate XML documents against a given schema as part of your INSERT or IMPORT operation, DB2 will automatically add type annotations to your XML documents.

3.3.2 Step 2: Registering the XML schema

Once you've created an appropriate XML schema, you need to register the schema with DB2. IBM provides multiple ways to do this. You can launch graphical wizards from the DB2 Control Center to guide you through the process, invoke system-supplied stored procedures, or issue DB2 commands directly. Let's use the latter method here, because it may help you more readily understand what DB2 is doing behind the scenes on your behalf.

If your schema is very large, you may need to increase your application heap size before attempting to register it. For example, issue the following statements shown in Example 3-6.

Example 3-6 Increasing the application heap size

```
connect to test;
update db cfg using applheapsz 10000;
```

Next, register your XML schema. If your XML schema does not reference other XML schemas, you may register and complete the process with a single command. Otherwise, you will need to issue individual commands to register your primary XML schema, add the other required schemas, and complete the registration process. When a schema document becomes very large, it's common to divide its content into multiple files to improve maintenance, readability, and reuse. This is akin to breaking up a complex application or component into multiple modules. For details on this topic, refer to the W3C "XML Schema primer". See "Resources" at the following Web site:

```
http://www-128.ibm.com/developerworks/db2/library/techarticle/dm-0603sa
racco/
```

This chapter uses a simple, independent XML schema. You can register it with DB2 using the following command shown in Example 3-7.

Example 3-7 Registering an XML schema

```
register xmlschema 'http://mysample.org' from 'C:/XMLFiles/ClientInfo.xsd' as
user1.mysample complete;
```

In this example, ClientInfo.xsd is the name of the XML schema file. It's located in the C:/XMLFiles directory. This XML schema will be registered in DB2's internal repository under the SQL schema "user1" and the XML schema "mysample." The http://mysample.org parameter is just a placeholder in this example. It specifies the uniform resource indicator (URI) referenced by XML instance documents; many XML documents use namespaces, which are specified using a URI. Finally, the "complete" clause will instruct DB2 to complete the XML schema registration process so that the schema may be used for validating XML data.

It's worth noting that the schema registration process doesn't involve specifying table columns to which the schema will be applied. In other words, schemas aren't the equivalent of SQL column constraints. A given schema can validate data for a variety of XML columns in different tables. However, validation isn't automatic. DB2 allows any well-formed XML document to be stored in an XML column. If you want to validate your data against a registered schema prior to storage, you need to instruct DB2 to do so.

3.3.3 Step 3: Importing XML data with validation

With an XML schema created and completely registered in DB2, you're now able to have DB2 validate XML data when inserting or importing it into a table. Let's revisit the earlier IMPORT scenario (see 3.2.2, "Using DB2 IMPORT" on page 34) with schema validation in mind.

If you've already populated your "clients" table, you might find it convenient to delete its contents or drop and recreate the table. This is only necessary if you plan to add the same data to the table as you did previously. Recall that "clients" was defined with a primary key on the client ID column, so attempting to import duplicate rows will fail.

To validate the XML data while importing it into the "clients" table, use the XMLVALIDATE clause of DB2 IMPORT. The following statement in Example 3-8 instructs DB2 to use your previously registered XML schema (user1.mysample) as the default XML Data Specifier (XDS) for validating the XML files specified in the clients.del file prior to inserting them into the "clients" table.

Example 3-8   Importing XML data with validation

```
import from clients.del of del xml from C:/XMLFILES
xmlvalidate using xds default user1.mysample
insert into user1.clients;
```

If DB2 determines that an XML document doesn't conform to the specified schema, the entire row associated with that document will be rejected. Figure 3-8 illustrates sample output from an IMPORT operation in which one row of six was rejected because its XML document didn't conform to the specified schema.

```
DB2 CLP

SQL3149N  "6" rows were processed from the input file.  "5" rows were
successfully inserted into the table.  "1" rows were rejected.

Number of rows read        = 6
Number of rows skipped     = 0
Number of rows inserted    = 5
Number of rows updated     = 0
Number of rows rejected    = 1
Number of rows committed   = 6
```

Figure 3-8   Sample output from DB2 IMPORT, with one row rejected

It's worth noting that XMLVALIDATE can also be used with INSERT statements
to instruct DB2 to validate XML data before inserting it. The syntax is similar to
the IMPORT example just shown, in that you specify a registered (and
completed) XML schema when invoking the XMLVALIDATE clause. For more
information about this, refer to "A simple Java example" at the following Web site:

```
http://www-128.ibm.com/developerworks/db2/library/techarticle/dm-0603sa
racco/sidefile1.html
```

3.4 Summary

DB2 9 provides significant new capabilities for supporting XML, including a new
XML data type and underlying engine-level components that automatically store
and process XML data in an efficient manner. To help you get up to speed
quickly on these features, this chapter described how to create a test database
and sample tables for storing XML documents. It also reviewed how you can
populate your database with XML data. Finally, it summarized DB2's ability to
validate XML data against user-supplied XML schemas and provided examples
to show you how to get started.

Now that you've learned how to store XML data using DB2's new "native" XML
capabilities, you're ready to query that data. You'll see how to do that in
subsequent chapters, which will introduce you to DB2's new XQuery support as
well as its XML extensions to SQL (sometimes called "SQL/XML").

Querying XML data with SQL

In this chapter, learn how to query data stored in XML columns using SQL and SQL/XML using DB2 9, (formerly codenamed "Viper"). A subsequent chapter (Chapter 5, "Querying XML data with XQuery" on page 63) will illustrate how to query XML data using XQuery, a new language supported by DB2.[1]

Although DB2's hybrid architecture represents a significant departure from previous releases, exploiting its new XML capabilities doesn't have to be a painful process. If you're already familiar with SQL, you can immediately apply your skills to working with XML data stored natively in DB2. See how in this chapter.

You may be surprised to learn that DB2 also supports "bilingual" queries – that is, queries that combine expressions from both SQL and XQuery. Which language (or combination of languages) you should use depends on your application needs, as well as your skills. Combining elements of two query languages into one query isn't as tough as you may think. And doing so can offer you powerful capabilities for searching and integrating traditional SQL and XML data.

---

[1] Information in this chapter was originally published as "Query DB2 XML data with SQL" by C. M. Saracco in IBM developerWorks, March 2006.

`http://www-128.ibm.com/developerworks/db2/library/techarticle/dm-0603sa racco2/`

© Copyright IBM Corp. 2006. All rights reserved.

4.1 Sample database

The queries in this chapter will access the sample tables created in Chapter 3, "Get off to a fast start with pureXML" on page 29. As a quick review, the sample "items" and "clients" tables are defined as shown in Example 4-1.

Example 4-1   Table definitions

```
create table items (
id                  int primary key not null,
brandname           varchar(30),
itemname            varchar(30),
sku                 int,
srp                 decimal(7,2),
comments    xml

create table clients(
id                  int primary key not null,
name                varchar(50),
status              varchar(10),
contactinfo         xml
)
```

Sample XML data included in the "items.comments" column is shown in Figure 4-1, while sample XML data included in the "clients.contactinfo" column is shown in Figure 4-2. Subsequent query examples will reference specific elements in one or both of these XML documents.

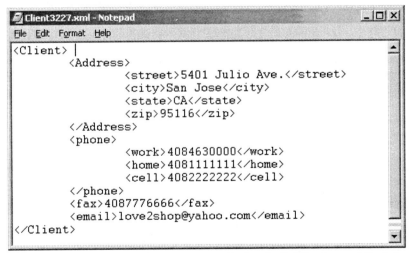

```
Comment3926.xml - Notepad                                              _□x
File  Edit  Format  Help
<Comments>
        <Comment>
                <CommentID>133</CommentID>
                <ProductID>3926</ProductID>
                <CustomerID>8877</CustomerID>
                <Message>Heels on shoes wear out too quickly.</Message>
                <ResponseRequested>No</ResponseRequested>
        </Comment>
        <Comment>
                <CommentID>514</CommentID>|
                <ProductID>3926</ProductID>
                <CustomerID>3227</CustomerID>
                <Message>Where can I find a supplier in San Jose?</Message>
                <ResponseRequested>Yes</ResponseRequested>
        </Comment>
</Comments>
```

Figure 4-1   Sample XML document stored in "comments" column of "items" table

```
Client3227.xml - Notepad                                _□x
File  Edit  Format  Help
<Client> |
        <Address>
                <street>5401 Julio Ave.</street>
                <city>San Jose</city>
                <state>CA</state>
                <zip>95116</zip>
        </Address>
        <phone>
                <work>4084630000</work>
                <home>4081111111</home>
                <cell>4082222222</cell>
        </phone>
        <fax>4087776666</fax>
        <email>love2shop@yahoo.com</email>
</Client>
```

Figure 4-2   Sample XML document stored in "contactinfo" column of the "clients" table

4.2 Query environment

All the queries in this chapter are designed to be issued interactively, which you can do through the DB2 command line processor or the DB2 Command Editor of the DB2 Control Center. The screen images and instructions in this chapter focus on the latter. (DB2 9 also ships with an Eclipse-based Developer Workbench that can help programmers graphically construct queries. However, this chapter does not discuss application development issues or the Developer Workbench.)

To use the DB2 Command Editor, launch the Control Center and select **Tools** → **Command Editor**. A window similar to Figure 4-3 will appear. Type your queries in the upper pane, click on the green arrow in the upper left corner to run them, and view your output in the lower pane or in the separate "Query results" tab.

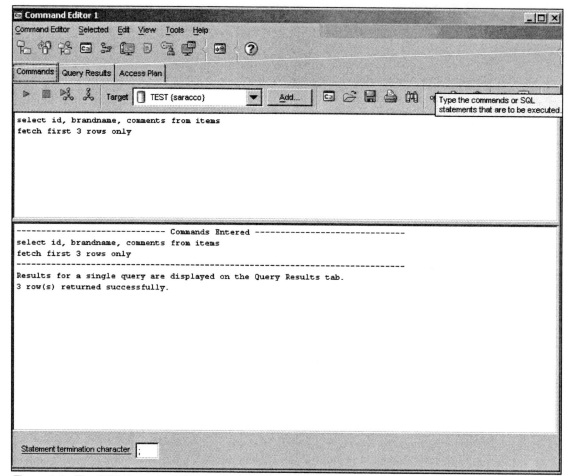

Figure 4-3   The DB2 Command Editor, which can be launched from the DB2 Control Center

4.3 SQL-only queries

Even if your knowledge of SQL is limited, you'll still be able to query XML data with little effort. For example, the following query (Example 4-2) selects the full contents of the "clients" table, including the XML information stored in the "contactinfo" column.

Example 4-2   Simple SELECT statement

```
select * from clients
```

Of course, you can write more selective SQL queries that incorporate relational projection and restriction operations. The following query (Example 4-3) retrieves the IDs, names, and contact information for all customers with a "Gold" status. Note that "contactinfo" contains XML data, while the other two columns do not.

Example 4-3   Simple SELECT statement with projection and restriction

```
select id, name, contactinfo
from clients
where status = 'Gold'
```

And, as you might expect, you can create views based upon such queries, as seen here with "goldview" (Example 4-4).

Example 4-4   Creating a view that contains an XML column

```
create view goldview as
select id, name, contactinfo
from clients
where status = 'Gold'
```

Unfortunately, there's a lot you cannot do with just SQL. Plain SQL statements enable you to retrieve full XML documents (as you've just seen), but you cannot specify XML-based query predicates and you cannot retrieve partial XML documents or specific element values from an XML document. In other words, you cannot project, restrict, join, aggregate, or order by fragments of XML documents using plain SQL. For example, you cannot retrieve just the e-mail addresses of your Gold customers or the names of clients who live in zip code "95116." To express these types of queries, you need to use SQL with XML extensions (SQL/XML), XQuery, or a combination of both.

The next section explores several fundamental features of SQL/XML. And in Chapter 5, "Querying XML data with XQuery" on page 63, learn how to write XQuery as well as how to combine XQuery with SQL.

4.4 SQL/XML queries

As the name implies, SQL/XML is designed to bridge between the SQL and XML worlds. It evolved as part of the SQL standard effort and now includes specifications for embedding XQuery or XPath expressions within SQL statements. XPath is a language for navigating XML documents to find elements or attributes. XQuery includes support for XPath.

It's important to note that XQuery (and XPath) expressions are case-sensitive. For example, XQuery that references the XML element "zip" will not apply to XML elements named "ZIP" or "Zip." Case sensitivity is sometimes difficult for SQL programmers to remember, because SQL query syntax permits them to use "zip," "ZIP," and "Zip" to refer to the same column name.

DB2 9 features more than 15 SQL/XML functions that enable you to search for specific data within XML documents, convert relational data into XML, convert XML data into relational data, and perform other useful tasks. This chapter does not cover the full breadth of SQL/XML. However, it reviews several common query challenges and how key SQL/XML functions can address these challenges.

4.4.1 "Restricting" results based on XML element values

SQL programmers often write queries that restrict the rows returned from the DBMS based on some condition. For example, the SQL query in Example 4-3 restricts the rows retrieved from the "clients" table to include only those customers with a "Gold" status. In this case, the customer's status is captured in an SQL VARCHAR column. But what if you want to restrict your search based on some condition that applies to data in an XML column? The XMLExists function of SQL/XML provides one means to do this.

XMLExists enables you to navigate to an element within your XML document and test for a specific condition. When specified as part of the WHERE clause, XMLExists restricts the returned results to only those rows that contain an XML document with the specific XML element value (in other words, where the specified value evaluates to "true").

Let's look at a sample query problem raised earlier. Imagine that you need to locate the names of all clients who live in a specific zip code. As you may recall, the "clients" table stores customers' addresses (including zip codes) in an XML column. (See Figure 4-2 on page 45.) Using XMLExists, you can search the XML column for the target zip code and restrict the returned result set accordingly. The following SQL/XML query (Example 4-5) returns the names of clients who live in zip code 95116.

Example 4-5   Restricting results based on an XML element value

```
select name from clients
where xmlexists('$c/Client/Address[zip="95116"]'
passing clients.contactinfo as "c")
```

The first line is an SQL clause specifying that you only want to retrieve information in the "name" column of the "clients" table. The WHERE clause invokes the XMLExists function, specifying an XPath expression that prompts DB2 to navigate to the "zip" element and check for a value of 95116. The "$c/Client/Address" clause indicates the path in the XML document hierarchy where DB2 can locate the "zip" element. Using data accessible from node "$c" (which we'll explain shortly), DB2 will navigate through the "Client" element to its "Address" sub-element to inspect zip code ("zip" values). The final line resolves the value of "$c": it's the "contactinfo" column of the "clients" table. Thus, DB2 inspects the XML data contained in the "contactinfo" column, navigates from the root "Client" element to "Address" and then to "zip," and determines if the customer lives in the target zip code. If so, the XMLExists function evaluates to "true," and DB2 returns the name of the client associated with that row.

A common mistake involves formulating the XMLExists query predicate, as shown in Example 4-6.

Example 4-6   Incorrect syntax for restricting results based on an XML element value

```
select name from clients
where xmlexists('$c/Client/Address/zip="95116" '
passing clients.contactinfo as "c")
```

While this query will execute successfully, it will not restrict the results to clients living in zip code 95116. (This is due to the semantics specified in the standard; it's not unique to DB2.) To restrict results to clients living in zip code 95116, you need to use the syntax shown earlier in Example 4-5.

You may be curious how to include a query that restricts XML data in an application. While this chapter does not discuss application development topics in detail, we include a simple Java example that uses a parameter marker within an SQL/XML statement to restrict output to information about customers who live in a given zip code. You can find this example at the following Web site:

```
http://www-128.ibm.com/developerworks/db2/library/techarticle/dm-0603sa
racco2/sidefile1.html
```

4.4.2 "Projecting" XML element values

Now let's consider a slightly different situation, in which you want to project XML values into your returned result set. In other words, we want to retrieve one or more element values from our XML documents. There are multiple ways to do this. Let's first use the XMLQuery function to retrieve a value for one element, and then use the XMLTable function to retrieve values for multiple elements and map these into columns of an SQL result set.

Let's consider how to solve a problem posed earlier: how to create a report listing the e-mail addresses of the Gold customers. The following query in Example 4-7 invokes the XMLQuery function to accomplish this task.

Example 4-7 Retrieving e-mail information for qualifying customers

```
select xmlquery('$c/Client/email'
passing contactinfo as "c")
from clients
where status = 'Gold'
```

The first line specifies that you want to return values for the "email" sub-element of the root "Client" element. The second and third lines indicate where DB2 can find this information – in the "contactinfo" column of the "clients" table. The fourth line further qualifies your query to indicate that you're only interested in e-mail addresses of Gold customers. This query will return a set of XML elements and values. For example, if you had 500 Gold customers, each with one e-mail address, your output would be a one-column result set with 500 rows, as shown in Example 4-8.

Example 4-8 Sample output for previous query

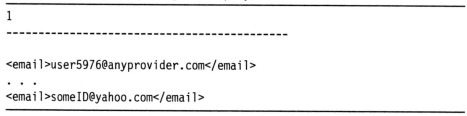

```
1
-------------------------------------------

<email>user5976@anyprovider.com</email>
. . .
<email>someID@yahoo.com</email>
```

If you have multiple e-mail addresses for individual Gold customers, you may want to instruct DB2 to return only the primary address (that is, the first e-mail address found in the customer's "contactinfo" document). You can modify the XPath expression in the first line of your query to do so, see Example 4-9.

```
select xmlquery('$c/Client/email[1]'
passing contactinfo as "c")
from clients
where status = 'Gold'
```

Finally, if you lack e-mail addresses for some Gold customers, you may want to write a query to exclude nulls from the result set. To do so, modify the previous query by adding another predicate to the WHERE clause to test for missing e-mail information. You're already familiar with the SQL/XML function that enables you to do that – it's XMLExists. Example 4-10 shows how you can rewrite the previous query to filter out any rows for Gold customers whose contact information (stored as XML) lacks an e-mail address.

Example 4-10   Retrieving the first e-mail address for each qualifying customer for whom we have at least one e-mail address

```
select xmlquery('$c/Client/email[1]'
passing contactinfo as "c")
from clients
where status = 'Gold'
and xmlexists('$c/Client/email' passing contactinfo as "c")
```

Now let's consider a slightly different situation, in which you need to retrieve multiple XML element values. XMLTable generates tabular output from data stored in XML columns and is quite useful for providing programmers with a "relational" view of XML data. Like XMLExists and XMLQuery, the XMLTable function causes DB2 to navigate through the XML document hierarchy to locate the data of interest. However, XMLTable also includes clauses to map the target XML data into result set columns of SQL data types.

Consider the following query (Example 4-11), which projects columns from both relational data and XML data stored in the "items" table. (See Figure 4-1 on page 45 to review the "items" table.) The comment IDs, customer IDs, and messages are stored in XML documents in the "comments" column. The item names are stored in an SQL VARCHAR column.

Example 4-11   Retrieving multiple XML elements and converting each to a traditional SQL data type

```
select t.Comment#, i.itemname, t.CustomerID, Message from items i,
xmltable('$c/Comments/Comment' passing i.comments as "c"
columns Comment# integer path 'CommentID',
    CustomerID integer path 'CustomerID',
    Message varchar(100) path 'Message') as t
```

The first line specifies the columns to be included in your result set. Columns surrounded by quotation marks and prefixed with the "t" variable are based on XML element values, as the subsequent lines of the query indicate. The second line invokes the XMLTable function to specify the DB2 XML column containing the target data ("i.comments") and the path within the column's XML documents where the elements of interest are located (within the "Comment" sub-element of the root "Comments" element). The "columns" clause, spanning lines 3 to 5, identifies the specific XML elements that will be mapped to output columns in the SQL result set, specified on line 1. Part of this mapping involves specifying the data types to which the XML element values will be converted. In this example, all XML data is converted to traditional SQL data types.

Figure 4-4 shows sample results from running this query. As you can see, the output is a simple SQL result set. Note that the column names have been folded into upper case – a normal occurrence with SQL.

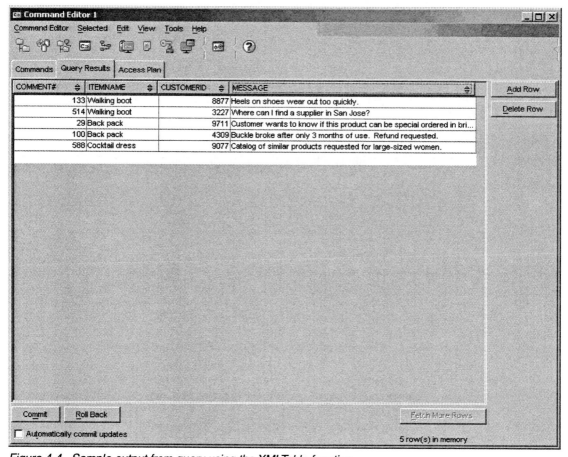

Figure 4-4   Sample output from query using the XMLTable function

If desired, you can use XMLTable to create result sets that include XML columns as well. For example, the following statement (Example 4-12) produces a result set similar to the previous one, except that "Message" data is contained in an XML column rather than an SQL VARCHAR column.

Example 4-12   Retrieving multiple XML elements and converting them to traditional SQL or XML data types

```
select t.Comment#, i.itemname, t.CustomerID, Message from items i,
xmltable('$c/Comments/Comment' passing i.comments as "c"
columns Comment# integer path 'CommentID',
   CustomerID integer path 'CustomerID',
   Message XML by ref path 'Message') as t
```

4.4.3 Creating relational views of XML data

As you might imagine, SQL/XML functions can be used to define views. This is particularly useful if you'd like to present your SQL application programmers with a relational model of data stored in XML columns.

Creating a relational view over data in an XML column isn't much more complicated than projecting XML element values. You simply write an SQL/XML SELECT statement that invokes the XMLTable function and use this as a basis for your view definition. The following example (Example 4-13) creates a view based on information in XML and non-XML columns of the "items" table. (It's similar to the query in Example 4-11 on page 51.)

Example 4-13   Creating a view, based on the output of XMLTable

```
create view commentview(itemID, itemname, commentID, message,
mustrespond) as
select i.id, i.itemname, t.CommentID, t.Message, t.ResponseRequested
from items i,
xmltable('$c/Comments/Comment' passing i.comments as "c"
columns CommentID integer path 'CommentID',
   Message varchar(100) path 'Message',
   ResponseRequested varchar(100) path 'ResponseRequested') as t;
```

Although it's easy to create relational views over XML column data, you should consider their use carefully. DB2 doesn't use XML column indexes when queries are issued against such views. Thus, if you indexed the ResponseRequested element and issued an SQL query that restricted the results of the "mustrespond" column to a certain value, DB2 would read all the XML documents and search for the appropriate "ResponseRequested" value. Unless you have a small amount of data, this would slow runtime performance. However, if the queries you plan to run against such views also contain highly restrictive predicates involving indexed columns of traditional SQL types ("i.id" or "i.itemname" in this example), you can mitigate potential runtime performance problems. DB2 uses the relational indexes to filter qualifying rows to a small number, and then applies any additional XML query predicates to these interim results before returning the final result set.

4.4.4 Joining XML and relational data

By now, you may be wondering about joining XML data with non-XML data (relational data based on traditional SQL types, for example). DB2 enables you to do this with a single SQL/XML statement. While there are different ways to formulate such joins, depending on your database schema and workload requirements, we'll cover one example here. And you may be surprised to learn that you already know enough about SQL/XML to get the job done.

Recall that the XML column in the "items" table contains a "CustomerID" element. This can serve as a join key for the integer-based "id" column in the "clients" table. So, if you want a report of the names and status of clients who've commented on one or more of your products, you'd have to join XML element values from one table with SQL integer values from another. And one way to accomplish this is to use the XMLExists function, as shown in Example 4-14.

Example 4-14 Joining XML and non-XML data

```
select clients.name, clients.status from items, clients
where xmlexists('$c/Comments/Comment[CustomerID=$p]'
passing items.comments as "c", clients.id as "p")
```

The first line identifies the SQL columns to be included in the query result set and the source tables referenced in the query. The second line includes your join clause. Here, XMLExists determines if the "CustomerID" value in one target source is equal to a value derived from another target source. The third line specifies these sources: the first is the "comments" XML column in the "items" table, and the second is the integer "id" column in the "clients" table. Thus, if customers have commented on any item and information about this customer is available in the "clients" table, the XMLExists expression will evaluate to "true" and the client's name and status information will be included in the report.

4.4.5 Using "FLWOR" expressions in SQL/XML

Although we've only discussed a few functions, SQL/XML provides many powerful capabilities for querying XML data and integrating that data with relational data. Indeed, you've already seen some examples of how to do that, but we'll discuss a few more here.

Both the XMLExists and XMLQuery functions enable you to incorporate XQuery into SQL. Our previous examples show how to use these functions with simple XPath expressions to navigate to a portion of an XML document of interest. Now let's consider a simple example in which you include XQuery in your SQL queries.

XQueries may contain some or all of the following clauses: **for**, **let**, **where**, **order by**, and **return**. Collectively, they form FLWOR (pronounced flower) expressions. SQL programmers may find it convenient to incorporate XQueries into their SELECT lists to extract (or project) fragments of XML documents into their result sets. And while that's not the only way the XMLQuery function can be used, it's the scenario this chapter covers. (Chapter 5, "Querying XML data with XQuery" on page 63 will discuss XQuery in greater depth.)

Let's imagine that you want to retrieve the names and primary e-mail addresses of your "Gold" customers. In some respects, this task is similar to one we undertook earlier (see Example 4-9 on page 51), when we explored how to project XML element values. Here, you pass XQuery (with **for** and **return** clauses) as input to the XMLQuery function. See Example 4-15.

Example 4-15   Retrieving XML data using **for** *and* **return** *clauses of XQuery*

```
select name, xmlquery('for $e in $c/Client/email[1] return $e'
passing contactinfo as "c")
from clients
where status = 'Gold'
```

The first line specifies that customer names and output from the XMLQuery function will be included in the result set. The second line indicates that the first "email" sub-element of the "Client" element is to be returned. The third line identifies the source of our XML data – the "contactinfo" column. Line 4 tells us that this column is in the "clients" table. Finally, the fifth line indicates that only "Gold" customers are of interest to us.

Because this example was so simple, you could write the same query here. Instead, you could write the same query in a more compact manner, much as you did previously. See Example 4-16.

Example 4-16   Rewriting the previous query in a more compact manner

```
select name, xmlquery('$c/Client/email[1]'
passing contactinfo as "c")
from clients
```

```
where status = 'Gold'
```

However, the **return** clause of XQuery enables you to transform XML output as needed. For example, you can extract e-mail element values and publish these as HTML. The following query (Example 4-17) will produce a result set in which the first e-mail address of each Gold customer is returned as an HTML paragraph.

Example 4-17   Retrieving and transforming XML into HTML

```
select xmlquery('for $e in $c/Client/email[1]/text()
return <p>{$e}</p>'
passing contactinfo as "c")
from clients
where status = 'Gold'
```

The first line indicates that you're interested in the text representation of the first e-mail address of qualifying customers. The second line specifies that this information is to be surrounded by HTML paragraph tags before it is returned. In particular, the curly brackets ({ }) instruct DB2 to evaluate the enclosed expression (in this case, "$e") rather than treat it as a literal string. If you omit the curly brackets, DB2 would return a result set containing "<p>$e</p>" for every qualifying customer record.

4.4.6 Publishing relational data as XML

Up until now, we've concentrated on ways to query, extract, or transform data contained within a DB2 XML column. And, as you've seen, these capabilities are all available through SQL/XML.

SQL/XML provides other handy features as well. Among these is the ability to convert or publish relational data as XML. This chapter only covers three SQL/XML functions in this regard: XMLElement, XMLAgg, and XMLForest.

XMLElement lets you convert data stored in traditional SQL columns into XML fragments. That is, you can construct XML elements (with or without XML attributes) from your base SQL data. The following example (Example 4-18) nests its use of the XMLElement function to create a series of item elements, each of which contains sub-elements for the ID, brand name, and stock-keeping unit ("sku") values obtained from the "items" table.

Example 4-18   Using XMLElement to publish relational data as XML

```
select xmlelement (name "item",
           xmlelement (name "id", id),
           xmlelement (name "brand", brandname),
           xmlelement (name "sku", sku) ) from items
where srp < 100
```

Running this query will produce a result similar to Example 4-19.

Example 4-19   Sample output from previous query

```
<item>
  <id>4272</id>
  <brand>Classy</brand>
  <sku>981140</sku>
</item>
. . .
<item>
  <id>1193</id>
  <brand>Natural</brand>
  <sku>557813</sku>
</item>
```

You can combine XMLElement with other SQL/XML publishing functions to construct and group XML values together, nesting them in hierarchies as desired. Example 4-20 uses XMLElement to create customerList elements whose contents are grouped by values in the "status" column. For each "customerList" record, the XMLAgg function returns a sequence of customer elements, each of which includes sub-elements based on our "name" and "status" columns. Furthermore, you see that customer element values are ordered by customer name.

Example 4-20   Aggregating and grouping data

```
select xmlelement(name "customerList",
xmlagg (xmlelement (name "customer",
xmlforest (name as "fullName", status as "status") )
order by name ) )
from clients
group by status
```

Let's assume our "clients" table contains three distinct "status" values: "Gold," "Silver," and "Standard." Running the previous query will cause DB2 to return three customerList elements, each of which may contain multiple customer sub-elements that further contain name and status information. Thus, the output will appear similar to Example 4-21.

Example 4-21   Sample output from previous query

```
<customerList>
  <customer>
    <fullName>Chris Bontempo</fullname>
    <status>Gold</status>
  </customer>
  <customer>
    <fullName>Ella Kimpton</fullName>
    <status>Gold</status>
  </customer>
. . .
</customerList>
<customerList>
  <customer>
    <fullName>Lisa Hansen</fullName>
    <status>Silver</status>
  </customer>
. . .
</customerList>
<customerList>
  <customer>
    <fullName>Rita Gomez</fullName>
    <status>Standard</status>
  </customer>
. . .
</customerList>
```

4.5 Update and delete operations

Although the focus of this chapter is on searching and retrieving data stored in XML columns using SQL, it's worth spending a few moments considering two other common tasks: updating and deleting data in XML columns.

DB2 enables users to update and delete XML data using SQL and SQL/XML statements. Indeed, because the initial draft of the XQuery standard does not address these issues, DB2 users must rely on SQL for these tasks.

4.5.1 Updating XML data

DB2 enables you to update an XML column with an SQL UPDATE statement or through the use of a system-supplied stored procedure (DB2XMLFUNCTIONS.XMLUPDATE). In both cases, updates to the XML column occur at a document level rather than an element level. However, programmers who update using the stored procedure do not need to supply the full XML document to DB2; they only need to specify the XML elements to be updated, and DB2 preserves the unchanged document data as well as updates the specified elements. Programmers issuing UPDATE statements need to specify the full document (not just the elements they want to change).

For example, if you want to issue an UPDATE statement to change the e-mail address of a particular client's contact information, you have to supply the full set of contact information to be included in the XML column, not just the new e-mail element value. Referring to Figure 4-2 on page 45, this would include "Address" information, "phone" information, "fax" information, and "email" information.

Consider the following statement shown in Example 4-22.

Example 4-22   Sample UPDATE statement

```
update clients set contactinfo=(
xmlparse(document '<email>newemail@someplace.com</email>' ) )
where id = 3227
```

If you recall how we inserted XML data in Chapter 3, "Get off to a fast start with pureXML" on page 29, much of this statement should look familiar. Like any SQL UPDATE statement, this example first identifies the table and column to be updated. Because the target column contains XML data, you need to supply a well-formed XML document as the new target value. While most production environments use host variables or parameter markers in applications to update their XML data, I've shown a simple way to do so interactively. The second line uses the XMLParse function to convert the input string into XML. Explicitly invoking XMLParse, as we do here, is optional with DB2 9. The final line is a standard SQL clause restricting the update to a particular row in your table.

If you execute the previous UPDATE statement, the "contactinfo" column for customer 3227 would contain only e-mail information, as shown in Example 4-23.

Example 4-23   Effect of executing previous UPDATE statement

```
<email>newemail@someplace.com</email>
```

The address, phone numbers, and fax number for this customer (shown in Figure 4-2 on page 45) would be lost. Furthermore, some of the earlier queries you wrote to extract the e-mail addresses of customers would never pick up this one. Why? The earlier queries included XPath or XQuery expressions that navigated through a specific document hierarchy in which Client was the root element and email was a sub-element. After updating this document as shown, email would now be the root element for this customer's XML record; therefore, its value wouldn't be found at the expected location in the hierarchy.

If you want to update this customer's e-mail address interactively and retain all other existing contact information, rewrite your query, as shown in Example 4-24.

Example 4-24   Revised UPDATE statement

```
update clients set contactinfo=
(xmlparse(document
''<Client>
   <Address>
      <street>5401 Julio Ave.</street>
      <city>San Jose</city>
      <state>CA</state>
      <zip>95116</zip>
   </Address>
   <phone>
      <work>4084633000</work>
      <home>4081111111</home>
      <cell>4082222222</cell>
   </phone>
   <fax>4087776666</fax>
   <email>newemail@someplace.com</email>
</Client>' ) )
where id = 3227
```

Perhaps you're wondering if you might be able to avoid supplying the full XML document by updating through a view. For example, the commentview defined in Example 4-13 on page 53 uses the XMLTable function to extract certain elements of an XML column and transform these into SQL columns in the view. Is it possible, then, to update the value of one of these SQL columns and have the result written back to the correct sub-element of the original XML document? No. DB2 distinguishes between view columns based on SQL types and view columns that are derived from the output of a function (in this case, the XMLTable function). Updates to the latter are not supported.

4.5.2 Deleting XML data

Deleting rows that contain XML columns is a straightforward process. The SQL DELETE statement enables you to identify (or restrict) the rows you want to delete through a WHERE clause. This clause may include simple predicates to identify non-XML column values or SQL/XML functions to identify XML element values contained within XML columns.

For example, here's how you can delete all customer information for customer ID 3227. See Example 4-25.

Example 4-25   Deleting data for a specific client

```
delete from clients
where id = 3227
```

Do you remember how to restrict SQL SELECT statements to return only rows for customers living in zip code 95116? If so, you can easily apply that knowledge to deleting rows that track those customers. Here's how to do so using XMLExists. See Example 4-26.

Example 4-26   Deleting data for clients within a specific zip code

```
delete from clients
where xmlexists('$c/Client/Address[zip="95116"]'
passing clients.contactinfo as "c");
```

4.5.3 Indexing

Finally, it's worth noting that you can create specialized XML indexes to speed up access to data stored in XML columns. Because this is an introductory chapter and the sample data is small, this chapter does not cover that topic here. However, in production environments, defining appropriate indexes can be critical to achieving optimal performance. The "Resources" section at the following Web site can help you learn more about new DB2 indexing technology:

```
http://www-128.ibm.com/developerworks/db2/library/techarticle/dm-0603sa
racco2/
```

4.6 Summary

This chapter covered a lot of ground, highlighting several key aspects of SQL/XML and how you can use it to query data in XML columns. There's certainly more you can do with SQL and SQL/XML functions than we've discussed here. This chapter includes a simple Java example that illustrates how you can use parameter markers with SQL/XML to query data in XML columns. Refer to the following Web site:

http://www-128.ibm.com/developerworks/db2/library/techarticle/dm-0603sa
racco2/sidefile1.html

We'll discuss application development issues in greater detail in Chapter 6, "Developing Java applications for XML data" on page 83. However, the next chapter will explore some interesting aspects of XQuery, a new query language supported by DB2 9.

Querying XML data with XQuery

In this chapter, learn how to query data stored in XML columns using XQuery.[1]

As you know, the new architecture of DB2 9, (formerly codenamed "Viper"), supports both tabular and hierarchical data structures. Indeed, previous chapters have summarized DB2's new XML features, described how to create database objects and populate them with XML data, and explained how to work with XML data using SQL and SQL/XML. This chapter continues to explore DB2 XML capabilities by focusing on its new support for XQuery.

DB2 treats XQuery as a first-class language, allowing users to write XQuery expressions directly rather than requiring that users embed or wrap XQueries in SQL statements. Furthermore, DB2 query engine processes XQueries natively, meaning that it parses, evaluates, and optimizes XQueries without ever translating them into SQL behind the scenes. Of course, if you choose to write "bilingual" queries that include both XQuery and SQL expressions, DB2 will process and optimize these queries as well.

---

[1] Information in this chapter was originally published as "Query DB2 XML data with XQuery" by D. Chamberlin, C. M. Saracco, IBM developerWorks, April 2006.

`http://www-128.ibm.com/developerworks/db2/library/techarticle/dm-0604sa racco/`

© Copyright IBM Corp. 2006. All rights reserved.

As with SQL/XML in Chapter 4, "Querying XML data with SQL" on page 43, this chapter reviews several common query tasks and looks at how you can use XQuery to accomplish your goals. But first, let's briefly consider how XQuery differs from SQL.

5.1 About XQuery

XQuery differs from SQL in a number of key respects, largely because the languages were designed to work with different data models that have different characteristics. XML documents contain hierarchies and possess an inherent order. Tabular data structures supported by SQL-based DBMSs are flat and set-based; as such, rows are unordered.

The differences between these data models result in a number of fundamental differences in their respective query languages. For example, XQuery supports path expressions to enable programmers to navigate through XML's hierarchical structure, while plain SQL (without XML extensions) does not. XQuery supports both typed and untyped data, while SQL data is always defined with a specific type. XQuery lacks null values because XML documents omit missing or unknown data. SQL, of course, uses nulls to represent missing or unknown data values. XQuery returns sequences of XML data; SQL returns result sets of various SQL data types.

These are just a subset of the fundamental differences between XQuery and SQL. It's beyond the scope of this introductory chapter to provide an exhaustive list, but an IBM Systems Journal paper discusses language differences in more detail. For more information, refer to the following Web site:

`http://www.research.ibm.com/journal/sj/452/ozcan.html`

For now though, let's just explore some basic aspects of the XQuery language and how you can use it to query XML data in DB2 9.

5.2 Sample database

The queries in this chapter access the sample tables created in Chapter 3, "Get off to a fast start with pureXML" on page 29. As a quick review, Example 5-1 defines the sample "items" and "clients" tables.

Example 5-1   Table definitions

```
create table items (
id              int primary key not null,
brandname       varchar(30),
itemname        varchar(30),
sku             int,
srp             decimal(7,2),
comments   xml
)
```

```
create table clients(
id              int primary key not null,
name            varchar(50),
status          varchar(10),
contactinfo     xml
)
```

Sample XML data included in the "items.comments" column is shown in
Figure 5-1, while sample XML data included in the "clients.contactinfo" column is
shown in Figure 5-2. Subsequent query examples will reference specific
elements in one or both of these XML documents.

```
Comment3926.xml - Notepad                                    _ □ ×
File  Edit  Format  Help
<Comments>
        <Comment>
                <CommentID>133</CommentID>
                <ProductID>3926</ProductID>
                <CustomerID>8877</CustomerID>
                <Message>Heels on shoes wear out too quickly.</Message>
                <ResponseRequested>No</ResponseRequested>
        </Comment>
        <Comment>
                <CommentID>514</CommentID>|
                <ProductID>3926</ProductID>
                <CustomerID>3227</CustomerID>
                <Message>Where can I find a supplier in San Jose?</Message>
                <ResponseRequested>Yes</ResponseRequested>
        </Comment>
</Comments>
```

Figure 5-1 Sample XML document stored in "comments" column of "items" table

```
Client3227.xml - Notepad                                    _ |□| x|
File  Edit  Format  Help
<Client> |
        <Address>
                <street>5401 Julio Ave.</street>
                <city>San Jose</city>
                <state>CA</state>
                <zip>95116</zip>
        </Address>
        <phone>
                <work>4084630000</work>
                <home>4081111111</home>
                <cell>4082222222</cell>
        </phone>
        <fax>4087776666</fax>
        <email>love2shop@yahoo.com</email>
</Client>
```

Figure 5-2   Sample XML document stored in "contactinfo" column of the "clients" table

5.3 Query environment

All the queries in this chapter are designed to be issued interactively. You can do this through the DB2 command line processor or the DB2 Command Editor of the DB2 Control Center. The screen images and instructions in this chapter focus on the latter. (DB2 9 also ships with an Eclipse-based Developer Workbench that can help programmers graphically construct queries. This chapter does not discuss application development issues or the Developer Workbench.)

To use the DB2 Command Editor, launch the Control Center, and select **Tools → Command Editor**. A window similar to Figure 5-3 will appear. Type your queries in the upper pane, click on the green arrow in the upper left corner to run them, and view your output in the lower pane or in the separate "Query Results" tab.

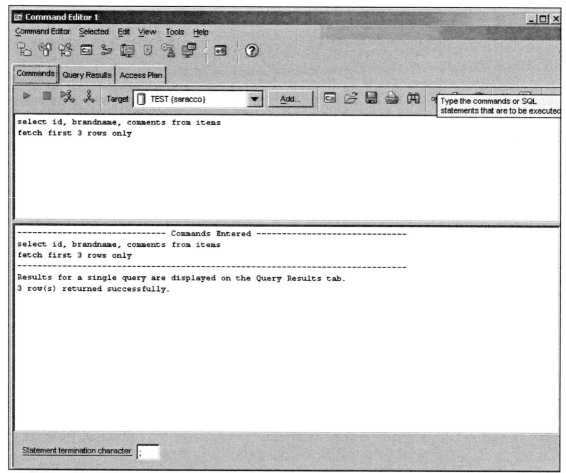

Figure 5-3 The DB2 Command Editor, which can be launched from the DB2 Control Center

5.4 XQuery examples

Just as in Chapter 4, "Querying XML data with SQL" on page 43, this chapter steps through several common business scenarios and shows how to use XQuery to satisfy requests for XML data. It also explores more complex situations that involve embedding SQL within XQuery.

XQuery provides several different kinds of expressions that may be combined in any way you like. Each expression returns a list of values that can be used as input to other expressions. The result of the outermost expression is the result of the query.

This chapter focuses on two important kinds of XQuery expressions: "FLWOR" expressions and path expressions. A FLWOR expression is much like a SELECT-FROM-WHERE expression in SQL: it is used to iterate through a list of items and to optionally return something that is computed from each item. A path expression, on the other hand, navigates through a hierarchy of XML elements and returns the elements that are found at the end of the path.

Like a SELECT-FROM-WHERE expression in SQL, an XQuery FLWOR expression may contain several clauses that begin with certain keywords. The following keywords are used to begin clauses in a FLWOR expression:

- **for**: Iterates through an input sequence, binding a variable to each input item in turn

- **let**: Declares a variable and assigns it a value, which may be a list containing multiple items

- **where**: Specifies criteria for filtering query results

- **order by**: Specifies the sort order of the result

- **return**: Defines the result to be returned

A path expression in XQuery consists of a series of "steps," separated by slash marks or characters (/). In its simplest form, each step navigates downward in an XML hierarchy to find the children of the elements returned by the previous step. Each step in a path expression may also contain a predicate that filters the elements that are returned by that step, retaining only elements that satisfy some condition. For example, assuming that the variable $clients is bound to a list of XML documents containing <Client> elements, the four-step path expression $clients/Client/Address[state = "CA"]/zip will return the list of zip codes for clients whose addresses are in California.

In many cases, it is possible to write a query by using either a FLWOR expression or a path expression.

5.4.1 Using DB2 XQuery as a top-level query language

To execute an XQuery directly in DB2 9 (as opposed to embedding it in an SQL statement), you must preface the query with the keyword **xquery**. This instructs DB2 to invoke its XQuery parser to process your request. Note that you only need to do this if you are using XQuery as the outermost (or top level) language. If you embed XQuery expressions in SQL, you do not need to preface them with the **xquery** keyword. However, this chapter uses XQuery as the primary language, so all the queries are prefaced with **xquery**.

When running as a top-level language, XQuery needs to have a source of input data. One way in which an XQuery can obtain input data is to call a function named db2-fn:xmlcolumn with a parameter that identifies the table name and column name of an XML column in a DB2 table. The db2-fn:xmlcolumn function returns the sequence (of XML documents) that is stored in the given column. For example, the following query (Example 5-2) returns a sequence of XML documents containing customer contact information.

Example 5-2   Simple XQuery to return customer contact data

```
xquery db2-fn:xmlcolumn('CLIENTS.CONTACTINFO')
```

As you may recall from our database schema (see 5.2, "Sample database" on page 65), we stored such XML documents in the "contactinfo" column of the "clients" table. Note that the column and table names are specified in upper case here. This is because table and column names are typically folded into upper case before being written to DB2's internal catalog. Because XQuery is case-sensitive, lower-case table and column names would fail to match upper-case names in the DB2 catalog.

5.4.2 Retrieving specific XML elements

Let's start with a basic task. Suppose you want to retrieve the fax numbers of all clients who have provided you with this information. Example 5-3 depicts one way you can write this query.

Example 5-3   FLWOR expression to retrieve client fax data

```
xquery
for $y in db2-fn:xmlcolumn('CLIENTS.CONTACTINFO')/Client/fax
return $y
```

The first line instructs DB2 to invoke its XQuery parser. The next line instructs DB2 to iterate through the fax sub-elements of the Client elements contained in the CLIENTS.CONTACTINFO column. Each fax element is bound in turn to the variable $y. The third line indicates that, for each iteration, the value of $y is returned. The result is a sequence of XML elements, as shown in Example 5-4.

Example 5-4   Sample output for previous query

```
<fax>4081112222</fax>
<fax>5559998888</fax>
```

As an aside, the output will also contain some information that's not of great interest in this chapter: XML version and encoding data, such as <?xml version="1.0" encoding="windows-1252" ?>, and XML namespace information, such as <fax xmlns:xsi="http://www.w3.org/2001/XMLSchema-instance">. To make the output easier for you to follow, we've omitted that information in this chapter. However, it can be important for a number of XML applications. If you use the DB2 command line processor to run your queries, you can use the **-d** option to suppress the XML declaration information and the **-i** option to print the results in an attractive manner.

The query shown in Example 5-3 could be expressed somewhat more concisely as a three-step path expression, as shown in Example 5-5.

Example 5-5   Path expression to retrieve client fax data

```
xquery
db2-fn:xmlcolumn('CLIENTS.CONTACTINFO')/Client/fax
```

The first step of the path expression calls the **db2-fn:xmlcolumn** function to obtain a list of XML documents from the CONTACTINFO column of the CLIENTS table. The second step returns all the Client elements in these documents, and the third step returns the fax elements nested inside these Client elements.

If you're not interested in obtaining XML fragments from your query but instead want just a text representation of qualifying XML element values, you can invoke the **text()** function in your **return** clause, as shown in Example 5-6.

Example 5-6   Two queries to retrieve text representation of client fax data

```
xquery
for $y in db2-fn:xmlcolumn('CLIENTS.CONTACTINFO')/Client/fax
return $y/text()

(or)

xquery
db2-fn:xmlcolumn('CLIENTS.CONTACTINFO')/Client/fax/text()
```

The output of these queries will be similar to that shown in Example 5-7.

Example 5-7   Sample output from previous queries

```
4081112222
5559998888
```

The results of the sample queries are relatively simple because the fax element is based on a primitive data type. Of course, elements may be based on complex types: that is, they may contain sub-elements (or nested hierarchies). The Address element of our client contact information is one example of this. According to the schema defined in Chapter 3, "Get off to a fast start with pureXML" on page 29, it may contain a street address, apartment number, city, state, and zip code. Consider what the following XQuery in Example 5-8 will return.

Example 5-8   FLWOR expression to retrieve complex XML type

```
xquery
for $y in db2-fn:xmlcolumn('CLIENTS.CONTACTINFO')/Client/Address
return $y
```

If you guessed a sequence of XML fragments containing Address elements and all their sub-elements, you're right (Example 5-9).

Example 5-9   Sample output from previous query

```
<Address>
  <street>5401 Julio Ave.</street>
  <city>San Jose</city>
  <state>CA</state>
  <zip>95116</zip>
</Address>
. . .
<Address>
  <street>1204 Meridian Ave.</street>
  <apt>4A</apt>
  <city>San Jose</city>
  <state>CA</state>
  <zip>95124</zip>
</Address>
```

> **Note:** This sample output is formatted to make it easier for you to read. The DB2 Command Editor displays each customer address record on one line.

5.4.3 Filtering on XML element values

You can refine the previous XQuery examples to be more selective. For example, let's explore how you can return the mailing addresses of all customers who live in zip code 95116.

As you might imagine, the XQuery **where** clause enables you to filter results based on the value of the zip element in your XML documents. Example 5-10 illustrates how to add a **where** clause to the previous FLWOR expression in Example 5-8 to obtain only the addresses that interest you.

*Example 5-10   FLWOR expression with a new **where** clause*

```
xquery
for $y in db2-fn:xmlcolumn('CLIENTS.CONTACTINFO')/Client/Address
where $y/zip="95116"
return $y
```

The added **where** clause is pretty easy to understand. The **for** clause binds the variable $y to each address in turn. The **where** clause contains a small path expression that navigates from each address to its nested zip element. The **where** clause is true (and the address is retained) only if the value of this zip element is equal to 95116.

The same result could be obtained by adding a predicate to the path expression, as shown in Example 5-11.

Example 5-11   Path expression with additional filtering predicate

```
xquery
db2-fn:xmlcolumn('CLIENTS.CONTACTINFO')/Client/Address[zip="95116"]
```

Of course, you can filter on zip code values and return elements unrelated to street addresses. Furthermore, you can also filter on multiple XML element values in a single query. The following query (Example 5-12) returns e-mail information for customers who live in a specific zip code in New York City (10011) or anywhere in the city of San Jose.

Example 5-12   Filtering on multiple XML element values with a FLWOR expression

```
xquery
for $y in db2-fn:xmlcolumn('CLIENTS.CONTACTINFO')/Client
where $y/Address/zip="10011" or $y/Address/city="San Jose"
return $y/email
```

Note that we've changed the **for** clause so that it binds variable $y to Client elements rather than to Address elements. This enables us to filter the Client elements by one part of the subtree (Address) and return another part of the subtree (email). The path expressions in the **where** clause and **return** clause must be written relative to the element that is bound to the variable (in this case, $y).

The same query can be expressed somewhat more concisely as a path expression. See Example 5-13.

Example 5-13   Filtering on multiple XML element values with a path expression

```
xquery
db2-fn:xmlcolumn('CLIENTS.CONTACTINFO')/Client[Address/zip="10011"
or Address/city="San Jose"]/email;
```

What's not so obvious from reviewing either form of this query is that the returned results will differ in two significant ways from what an SQL programmer might expect:

► You won't get XML data returned for qualifying customers who didn't give you their e-mail addresses. In other words, if you have 1000 customers who live in San Jose or zip code 10011, and 700 customers each gave you one e-mail address, you'd get a list of these 700 e-mail addresses returned. This is due to a fundamental difference between XQuery and SQL mentioned earlier -- XQuery doesn't use nulls.

► You won't know which e-mail addresses were derived from the same XML document. In other words, if you have 700 customers who live in San Jose or zip code 10011, and each gave you two e-mail addresses, you'd get a list of 1400 e-mail elements returned. You would not get a sequence of 700 records, each consisting of two e-mail addresses.

Both situations can be desirable under some circumstances and undesirable under others. For example, if you need to e-mail a notice to every qualifying account you have on record, then iterating through a list of customer e-mail addresses in XML format is easy to do in an application. However, if you want to e-mail only one notice to every customer, including those who only provided you with their street addresses, then the XQuery previously shown won't be sufficient.

There are multiple ways you can rewrite this query so that the returned results represent missing information in some fashion and indicate when multiple e-mail addresses were derived from the same customer record (that is, the same XML document). Let's explore one way shortly. However, if all you want to do is retrieve a list containing one e-mail address per qualifying customer, you could modify the **return** clause of the previous query slightly. See Example 5-14.

Example 5-14   Retrieving only the first e-mail element per customer

```
xquery
for $y in db2-fn:xmlcolumn('CLIENTS.CONTACTINFO')/Client
where $y/Address/zip="10011" or $y/Address/city="San Jose"
return $y/email[1]
```

This query causes DB2 to return the first e-mail element it finds within each qualifying XML document (customer contact record). If it doesn't find an e-mail address for a qualifying customer, it won't return anything for that customer.

5.4.4 Transforming XML output

A powerful aspect of XQuery is its ability to transform XML output from one form of XML into another. For example, you can use XQuery to retrieve all or part of your stored XML documents and convert the output into HTML for easy display in a Web browser. The following query in Example 5-15 retrieves the addresses of our clients, sorts the results by zip code, and converts the output into XML elements that are part of an unordered HTML list.

Example 5-15   Querying DB2 XML data and returning results as HTML

```
xquery
<ul> {
for $y in db2-fn:xmlcolumn('CLIENTS.CONTACTINFO')/Client/Address
order by $y/zip
return <li>{$y}</li>
} </ul>
```

The query begins simply enough with the **xquery** keyword to indicate to the DB2 parser that XQuery is being used as the primary language. The second line causes the HTML markup for an unordered list (<ul>) to be included in the results. It also introduces a curly bracket, the first of two sets used in this query. Curly brackets instruct DB2 to evaluate and process the enclosed expression rather than treat it as a literal string.

The third line iterates over client addresses, binding the variable $y to each address element in turn. The fourth line includes a new **order by** clause, specifying that results must be returned in ascending order (the default order) based on customer zip codes (the zip sub-element of each address bound to $y). The **return** clause indicates that the Address elements are to be surrounded by HTML list item tags before they are returned. And the final line concludes the query and completes the HTML unordered list tag.

The output will appear similar to that in Example 5-16.

Example 5-16   Sample HTML output of previous query

```
<ul>
  <li>
    <Address>
        <street>9407 Los Gatos Blvd.</street>
        <city>Los Gatos</city>
```

```
            <state>CA</state>
            <zip>95032</zip>
         </Address>
      </li>
      <li>
         <Address>
            <street>4209 El Camino Real</street>
            <city>Mountain View</city>
            <state>CA</state>
            <zip>95033</zip>
         </Address>
      </li>
   . . .
</ul>
```

Let's consider a topic raised earlier: how to write an XQuery that will indicate missing values in the returned results as well as indicate when a single XML document (such as a single customer record) contains repeating elements (such as multiple e-mail addresses). One way to do so involves wrapping the returned output in a new XML element, as shown in the following query in Example 5-17.

Example 5-17   Indicating missing values and repeating elements in an XQuery result

```
xquery
for $y in db2-fn:xmlcolumn('CLIENTS.CONTACTINFO')/Client
where $y/Address[zip="10011"] or $y/Address[city="San Jose"]
return <emailList> {$y/email} </emailList>
```

Running this query causes a sequence of "emailList" elements to be returned, one per qualifying customer record. Each emailList element will contain e-mail data. If DB2 finds a single e-mail address in a customer's record, it will return that element and its value. If it finds multiple e-mail addresses, it will return all e-mail elements and their values. Finally, if it finds no e-mail address, it will return an empty emailList element. Thus, the output might appear as shown in Example 5-18.

Example 5-18   Sample output of previous query

```
<emailList>
   <email>love2shop@yahoo.com</email>
</emailList>
<emailList/>
<emailList>
   <email>beatlesfan36@hotmail.com</email>
   <email>lennonfan36@hotmail.com</email>
```

```
</emailList>
. . .
```

5.4.5 Using conditional logic

XQuery's ability to transform XML output can be combined with its built-in
support for conditional logic to reduce the complexity of application code. Let's
consider a simple example. The "items" table includes an XML column
containing comments customers have made about products. For customers who
have requested a response to their comments, you may want to create new
"action" elements containing the product ID, customer ID, and message so you
can route this information to the appropriate person for handling. However,
comments that don't require a response are still important to the business, and
you don't want to just ignore them. Instead, create an "info" element with just the
product ID and message. Here's how you can use an XQuery **if-then-else**
expression to accomplish this task. See Example 5-19.

*Example 5-19   Using an **if-then-else** expression in an XQuery*

```
xquery
for $y in db2-fn:xmlcolumn('ITEMS.COMMENTS')/Comments/Comment
return (
        if ($y/ResponseRequested = 'Yes')
            then <action>
                        {$y/ProductID,
                         $y/CustomerID,
                         $y/Message}
                </action>
            else ( <info>
                        {$y/ProductID,
                         $y/Message}
                        </info>
    )
)
```

Most aspects of this query should be familiar to you by now, so let's just
concentrate on the conditional logic. The **if** clause determines whether the value
of the ResponseRequested sub-element for a given comment is equal to "Yes." If
so, the **then** clause is evaluated, causing DB2 to return a new element ("action")
that contains three sub-elements: ProductID, CustomerID, and Message.
Otherwise, the **else** clause is evaluated and DB2 returns an "info" element
containing only product ID and message data.

5.4.6 Using the "let" clause

You have now seen how to use all the parts of a FLWOR expression except for one: the let clause. This clause is used to assign a value (possibly containing a list of several items) to a variable that can be used in other clauses of the FLWOR expression.

Suppose that you want to make a list of how many comments were received for each product. This can be done with the following query (Example 5-20).

Example 5-20   Using the let clause

```
xquery
for $p in distinct-values
    (db2-fn:xmlcolumn('ITEMS.COMMENTS')/Comments/Comment/ProductID)
let $pc := db2-fn:xmlcolumn('ITEMS.COMMENTS')
      /Comments/Comment[ProductID = $p]
return
   <product>
         <id> { $p } </id>
         <comments> { count($pc) } </comments>
   </product>
```

The **distinct-values** function in the **for** clause returns a list of all the distinct values of ProductID that are found inside comments in the COMMENTS column of the ITEMS table. The **for** clause binds variable $p to each of these ProductID values in turn. For each value of $p, the **let** clause scans the ITEMS column again and binds the variable $pc to a list containing all the comments whose ProductID matches the ProductID in $p. The **return** clause constructs a new "product" element for each distinct ProductID value. Each of these "product" elements contains two sub-elements: an "id" element containing the ProductID value and a "comments" element containing a count of how many comments were received for the given product.

The result of this example query might look something like the one shown in Example 5-21.

Example 5-21   Sample output for the previous query

```
<product>
      <id>3926</id>
      <comments>28</comments>
</product>
<product>
```

```
        <id>4097</id>
        <comments>13</comments>
</product>
```

5.5 XQueries with embedded SQL

By now, you've seen how to write XQueries that retrieve XML document fragments, create new forms of XML output, and return different output based on conditions specified in queries themselves. In short, you've learned a few ways to use XQuery to query XML data stored in DB2.

To be sure, there's more to learn about XQuery than this brief chapter covers. But we cannot neglect a broad topic that we haven't covered yet: how to embed SQL within XQuery. Doing so can be useful if you need to write queries that filter data based on XML and non-XML column values.

As you might recall from Chapter 4, "Querying XML data with SQL" on page 43, the chapter described how you can embed simple XQuery expressions within an SQL statement to accomplish this task. Here, let's look at how to do the opposite: embed SQL within XQuery to restrict results based on both traditional SQL data values and specific XML element values.

In place of the **db2-fn:xmlcolumn** function, which returns all the XML data in a column of a table, you can call the **db2-fn:sqlquery** function, which executes an SQL query and returns only the selected data. The SQL query passed to **db2-fn:sqlquery** must return XML data. This XML data can then be further processed by XQuery.

The query in Example 5-22 retrieves information about comments involving products with a suggested retail price ("srp") of more than $100 that include a customer request for a response. Recall that pricing data is stored in an SQL decimal column, while customer comments are stored as XML. The returned data, including the product ID, customer ID, and customer message, is included in a single XML "action" element for each qualifying comment stored in the database.

Example 5-22 Embedding SQL within an XQuery

```
xquery
for $y in
db2-fn:sqlquery('select comments from items where srp >
100')/Comments/Comment
where $y/ResponseRequested="Yes"
return (
```

```
<action>
        {$y/ProductID,
         $y/CustomerID,
         $y/Message}
</action>
)
```

Again, most of this query should look familiar to you by now, so let's just concentrate on the new function: **db2-fn:sqlquery**. DB2 processes the SQL SELECT statement supplied to this function to determine which rows contain information about items priced at more than $100. The documents stored in these rows serve as inputs to a path expression that returns all the nested Comment elements. Subsequent portions of the query use the XQuery **where** clause to filter returned data further and to transform portions of the selected comments into new XML fragments.

With this in mind, let's consider how you might solve a slightly different problem. Imagine that you want a list of all e-mail addresses for "Gold" clients who live in San Jose. Furthermore, if you have multiple e-mail addresses for a single client, you want all of them to be included in the output as part of a single client record. Finally, if a qualifying "Gold" client didn't give you an e-mail address, you want to retrieve that client's mailing address. Example 5-23 illustrates one way to write such a query.

Example 5-23   Embedding SQL within an XQuery that includes conditional logic

```
xquery
for $y in
db2-fn:sqlquery('select contactinfo from clients where status=''Gold'' ')/Client
where $y/Address/city="San Jose"
return (
    if ($y/email) then <emailList>{$y/email}</emailList>
    else $y/Address
)
```

Two aspects of this query deserve some explanation. First, the SELECT statement embedded in the second line contains a query predicate based on the "status" column, comparing the value of this VARCHAR column to the string "Gold". In SQL, such strings are surrounded by single quotes. Note that although the example may appear to use double quotes, it actually uses two single quotes before and after the comparison value ("Gold"). The "extra" single quotes are escape characters. If you use double quotes around your string-based query predicate, instead of pairs of single quotes, you'll get a syntax error.

In addition, the **return** clause in this query contains conditional logic to determine if an e-mail element is present in a given customer's record. If so, the query will return a new "emailList" element containing all the customer's e-mail addresses (that is, all the e-mail elements for that customer). If not, it will return the customer's mailing address (that is, the Address element for that customer).

5.5.1 Indexing

Finally, it's worth noting that you can create specialized XML indexes to speed up access to data stored in XML columns. Because this is an introductory chapter and the sample data is small, we won't cover that topic here. However, in production environments, defining appropriate indexes can be critical to achieving optimal performance. See "Resources" at the following Web site for more info about DB2's new indexing technology:

```
http://www-128.ibm.com/developerworks/db2/library/techarticle/dm-0604sa
racco/
```

5.6 Summary

XQuery differs from SQL in significant ways, several of which are highlighted in this chapter. Learning more about the language will help you determine when it can be most beneficial to your work, as well as help you understand when it can be useful to combine XQuery with SQL. In Chapter 6, "Developing Java applications for XML data" on page 83, we'll delve into another topic you may find interesting: how to develop Java applications that exploit DB2 XML capabilities. For now though, refer to this simple Java example that depicts how a Java application might embed an XQuery.

► A simple Java coding example

```
http://www-128.ibm.com/developerworks/db2/library/techarticle/dm-060
3saracco2/sidefile1.html
```

6

Developing Java applications for XML data

In this chapter, you'll learn the basics of how to write Java applications that access the new XML data using DB2 9 (formerly codenamed "Viper"). You'll see how to insert, query, update, and delete XML data, as well as how to create stored procedures that access XML data, and more.[1]

Writing Java applications that access XML data stored natively in DB2 9 isn't much different from writing Java applications that access relational data. Indeed, if you're familiar with Java Database Connectivity (JDBC), you already know much of what you need to begin writing your first DB2 XML application.

In this chapter, we'll step through several common programming scenarios, such as inserting XML data, querying XML and non-XML data, updating XML data, deleting XML data, and creating stored procedures that access XML data. But first, let's review a few fundamental guidelines for developing any type of DB2 database application.

---

[1] Information in this chapter was originally published as "Develop Java applications for DB2 XML data", C. M. Saracco, IBM developerWorks, April 2006.

http://www-128.ibm.com/developerworks/db2/library/techarticle/dm-0605sa racco/

© Copyright IBM Corp. 2006. All rights reserved.

6.1 Follow typical programming "best practices"

Although DB2's pureXML support is new, good database application programming practices haven't changed. Before diving into the details of DB2's XML technology, keep these general principles in mind:

► Ask only for what you need: Do not retrieve the entire contents of a table – or the entire contents of many XML documents – if you only need a subset of this information. You'll just drive up processing costs and slow runtime performance.

► Avoid duplicating the work of a database server: Instruct DB2 to filter and process data according to your needs rather than doing this work in your application. For example, if you have DB2 return results in a specified order, you won't need to sort the data yourself. Similarly, if you have DB2 ensure that only distinct results are returned, you won't have to double-check for duplicates. Data-centric processing is best performed by the database server, not your application.

► Make your code easy to maintain: Include comments or Javadoc in your code, particularly if your application contains complex queries.

► Consider the scope of your transactions carefully: By default, JDBC treats each query as an independent transaction. Determine if this is appropriate for your needs, and also consider how the scope (and isolation level) you define for your transactions can impact overall concurrency requirements.

► Minimize traffic in networked environments: You'll enjoy better runtime performance if you avoid transferring data unnecessarily between your application and DB2. Retrieving only the data you need is one way to do this. Invoking database stored procedures can also help, depending on the nature of your work.

6.2 Configure your environment

DB2 doesn't require any special configuration to enable you to develop or run Java applications that work with XML data. Indeed, you can write, test, and debug your Java programs using the integrated development environment (IDE) of your choice or by working directly with a supported Java Developer Kit (JDK) from the command line. However, because DB2 9 ships with a Developer Workbench, the examples in this chapter use its development environment. This section discusses how to configure the Developer Workbench, reviews some sample data, and explores database configuration parameters that may be of interest to you.

6.2.1 DB2 Developer Workbench

The DB2 Developer Workbench is based on the Eclipse 3.1 platform, an open source project available for free download. To compile and run any DB2 XML application with this workbench, you need to create a project and include appropriate DB2 libraries in the project's build path, including the libraries that support DB2's JDBC 3.0-compliant driver. To configure your environment, complete the following steps:

1. Launch the DB2 Workbench. For example, from the Windows Start menu, select **DB2 → IBM DB2 Developer Workbench V9.1 → Developer Workbench**.

2. Create a new project. We'll use a simple project initially. Switch to the Java perspective (**Window → Open Perspective → Java**), and select **File → New → Project**. Follow the wizards to specify a project name. For other items, retain the default settings.

3. Add the DB2 libraries into your project's build path. Highlight your project, right-mouse click, and select **Properties**. Select **Java Build Path**, and click the **Libraries** tab. Add the appropriate DB2 external .jar files, such as db2jcc.jar, db2jcc_javax.jar, and db2jcc_license_cu.jar.

4. Optionally, create a package for your application. Highlight your project, right-mouse click and select **New → Package**.

For details about creating projects and packages, consult the online help information.

6.2.2 Sample data

The examples in this chapter work with the "clients" table created in Chapter 3, "Get off to a fast start with pureXML" on page 29. As a quick review, this table was defined as Example 6-1.

Example 6-1   Sample code listing at maximum width

```
create table clients(
   id              int primary key not null,
   name            varchar(50),
   status          varchar(10),
   contactinfo     xml
)
```

Figure 6-1 depicts a sample XML file that will be inserted into the "contactinfo" column of this table shortly.

```
Client1885.xml - Notepad
File  Edit  Format  View  Help
<?xml version="1.0"?>
<Client>
        <Address>
                <street>54 Moorpark Ave.</street>
                <city>San Jose</city>
                <state>CA</state>
                <zip>95110</zip>
        </Address>
        <phone>
                <work>4084630110</work>
                <home>4081114444</home>
                <cell>4082223333</cell>
        </phone>
        <fax>4087776688</fax>
        <email>sailer555@yahoo.com</email>
</Client>
```

Figure 6-1   Sample XML file to be inserted into the "clients" table

6.2.3 Database configuration parameters

The examples in this tutorial are simple and work with a small amount of XML data, so you shouldn't need to alter default database configuration parameters to get them to run. However, default values may not be sufficient for some production environments. In particular, settings for the log size, Java heap, query statement heap, and application heap may need to be increased. If these values are set inappropriately, your runtime performance may be slow or you may be unable to insert large XML documents into DB2 tables due to insufficient log space.

You can review and change DB2 database configuration parameters from the DB2 Control Center (select **Tools** → **Configuration Assistant**) or the DB2 command line processor. Consult the product manuals for details.

6.3 Connect to your database

Working with DB2 XML data requires establishing a connection to the database that contains your data. There's nothing special about this code: it's the same logic that you'd write to connect to any DB2 database.

Example 6-2 contains a helper class with methods for establishing and closing a DB2 database connection.

Example 6-2 Helper class to acquire and release database connections

```java
public class Conn {
   // for simplicity, I've hard-coded account and URL data.
   private static String user = "user1";
   private static String pwd = "mypassword";
   private static String url = "jdbc:db2:test";

   // this method gets a database connection
   public static Connection getConn(){
     Connection conn=null;

     //  load the appropriate DB2 driver and
     //  get a connection to the "test" database
     try {
        Class.forName("com.ibm.db2.jcc.DB2Driver");
        conn = DriverManager.getConnection(url, user, pwd);
        . . .
     }
     catch (Exception e) { e.printStackTrace();}
     return conn;

   }   // end getConn();

   // this method closes a database connection
   public static void closeConn(Connection conn){
     try {
       if(conn == null) { return; }
       conn.close();
     }
     catch (Exception e) { e.printStackTrace(); }
     finally {
       try { conn.close();  }
       catch (Exception e) { }
     }
   }  // end closeConn();
}  // end class
```

You will call these methods in applications that perform broader tasks, such as inserting and querying XML data.

6.4 Insert XML data

Because the initial XQuery specification did not address database write operations (such as inserting data), DB2 relies on familiar SQL INSERT statements to enable programmers to write new XML data to tables that contain XML columns. DB2 can store any well-formed XML document of up to 2 GB.

Often, Java programmers need to insert XML data contained in files into DB2, although it's also possible to insert XML data from character strings, from binary data (including large objects), and from SQL sub-select statements. A review of how to insert XML data from files and from simple character strings is provided here. Consult the DB2 9 manuals for details on other insert scenarios.

DB2 9 also enables you to insert XML documents with or without validating them against previously registered XML schemas. The samples in this chapter cover both approaches.

6.4.1 Insert file without validation

The `insertFile()` method in Example 6-3 illustrates how to insert data from an XML file into the "clients.contactinfo" column. This method begins by defining several variables for later use. The first three correspond to the ID, name, and status columns in the "clients" table. The fourth is the name of the XML file to be inserted into the "contactinfo" column. For simplicity, values have been hard-coded in this method; in a production environment, input values would be obtained differently.

After establishing a database connection, create a simple string for your INSERT statement. As you can see, it looks like any other DB2 INSERT statement and uses parameter markers for your four input column values. The INSERT statement is prepared as usual, and its four parameter markers are set. To set the marker for the XML column, open a FileInputStream, passing in the location of our XML file. Also obtain the length of this file, and use this information as input to the `setBinaryStream()` method. Finally, execute the statement, check for errors, and close the connection.

Example 6-3 Inserting XML data from a file

```
public static void insertFile(){
  try {
    // for simplicity, I've defined variables with input data
    int id = 1885;
    String name = "Amy Liu";
    String status = "Silver";
    String fn = "c:/XMLFiles/Client1885.xml";  // input file
```

```
// get a connection
Connection conn = Conn.getConn();

//   define string that will insert file without validation
String query = "insert into clients (id, name, status, contactinfo) values (?, ?, ? ,?)";

// prepare the statement
PreparedStatement insertStmt = conn.prepareStatement(query);
insertStmt.setInt(1, id);
insertStmt.setString(2, name);
insertStmt.setString(3, status);
File file = new File(fn);
insertStmt.setBinaryStream(4, new FileInputStream(file), (int)file.length());

// execute the statement
if (insertStmt.executeUpdate() != 1) {
    System.out.println("No record inserted.");
}
. . .
conn.close();
}
catch (Exception e) { . . . }
}
```

6.4.2 Insert file with validation

Inserting an XML file with validation requires very little additional programming effort. Assuming you have created and registered the ClientInfo.xsd file as discussed in Chapter 3, "Get off to a fast start with pureXML" on page 29, you only need to modify one line of code in Example 6-3 to instruct DB2 to insert the XML file with validation. This code involves the definition of the **query** string.

As shown in Example 6-4, the revised INSERT statement invokes the XMLValidate function before specifying a parameter marker for the XML data. This function also requires that you specify the XML schema identifier to be used for validation. Here, we refer to a previously-registered schema known as "user1.mysample".

Example 6-4   Inserting XML data from a file with validation

```
String query = "INSERT INTO clients (id, name, status contactinfo) " +
      "VALUES (?, ?, ?, xmlvalidate(? according to xmlschema id
user1.mysample))";
```

If your input XML file contains data that is valid according to the specified schema, DB2 inserts the row. If not, the entire statement fails, and no data for this row is inserted.

6.4.3 Insert character string without validation

The **insertString()** method shown in Example 6-5 illustrates how you can insert a well-formed XML document assigned to a character string variable into DB2. The logic is not much different from the previous example of inserting data from a file. Instead of using the **setBinaryStream()** method of your prepared statement, use the **setString()** method. For simplicity, the XML document in the **xml** variable definition has been hard-coded in this example.

> **Note:** Escape characters (backward slashes) are included before quotation marks that are part of the XML document (such as the XML version number in the example below).

Example 6-5   Inserting XML data from a character string

```
public static void insertString(){
  try {
    // for simplicity, I've defined variables with input data
    int id = 1885;
    String name = "Amy Liu";
    String status = "Silver";
    String xml =
      "<?xml version=\"1.0\"?>" +
      "<Client>" +
      "<Address> " +
        "<street>54 Moorpark Ave.</street>" +
        "<city>San Jose</city>" +
        "<state>CA</state>" +
        "<zip>95110</zip>" +
      "</Address>" +
      "<phone>" +
        "<work>4084630110</work>" +
        "<home>4081114444</home>" +
        "<cell>4082223333</cell>" +
      "</phone>" +
      "<fax>4087776688</fax>" +
      "<email>sailer555@yahoo.com</email>" +

    Connection conn = Conn.getConn();

    //   define string that will insert file without validation
    String query = "insert into clients (id, name, status, contactinfo) values (?, ?, ? ,?)";
```

```
  // prepare the statement
  PreparedStatement insertStmt = conn.prepareStatement(query);
  insertStmt.setInt(1, id);
  insertStmt.setString(2, name);
  insertStmt.setString(3, status);
  insertStmt.setString(4, xml);

  // execute the statement
  if (insertStmt.executeUpdate() != 1) {
      System.out.println("No record inserted.");
  }
  . . .
  conn.close();
}
catch (Exception e) { . . . }
}
```

6.4.4 Insert character string with validation

As you might expect, validating XML documents that are provided as character strings requires little extra programming effort. Indeed, only one line of code needs to be modified: the definition of the **query** variable. You simply need to change the INSERT statement to invoke the XMLValidate function, just as you did in Example 6-4.

Here's the revised statement shown in Example 6-6.

Example 6-6   Inserting XML data from a character string with validation

```
String query = "INSERT INTO clients (id, name, status contactinfo) " +
    "VALUES (?, ?, ?, xmlvalidate(? according to xmlschema id
user1.mysample))";
```

6.5 Query XML data

Now that you know how to insert XML data into DB2 using a Java program, you're ready to query XML data. There are several examples in this section to step through, starting with a simple task (such as retrieving a full XML document) and progressing to more difficult tasks (such as returning portions of XML documents based on XML and relational query predicates).

Although DB2 supports both SQL and XQuery as top-level languages, XQuery doesn't provide a means to resolve parameter markers. As a practical matter, this means that any XQueries in your application that require more than hard-coded query predicates must be wrapped in a SQL statement using a SQL/XML function, such as XMLQuery or XMLExists. Chapter 4, "Querying XML data with SQL" on page 43 discusses these functions in greater detail. Here, you'll see how to use them in a Java program. And, just for fun, you'll also see how to include an XQuery with hard-coded query predicates in an application.

6.5.1 Retrieve full XML documents

Our first query-based method is rather simple. It merely retrieves the full contact information for a given client. A query of this nature can be expressed easily in SQL. So, if you're familiar with JDBC, this code should be easy for you to understand.

The `simpleQuery()` method in Example 6-7 declares several variables and then establishes a database connection using a helper method defined in Example 6-2 on page 87. The **query** string contains a simple SQL statement to select all contact information for a specific client. After executing the statement, the application prints the results that have been fetched into a character string variable (stringDoc).

Example 6-7   Retrieving full XML documents with SQL

```
import java.sql.*;
 . . .
public static void simpleQuery() {
  PreparedStatement selectStmt = null;
  String query = null, stringDoc = null;
  ResultSet rs = null;
  int clientID = 1885;

  try{
     // get a connection
    Connection conn = Conn.getConn();

    // define, prepare, and execute the query
    // this will retrieve all XML data for a specific client
    query = "select contactinfo from clients where id = " + clientID
    selectStmt = conn.prepareStatement(query);
    rs = selectStmt.executeQuery();

    // check for results
    if (rs.next() == false) {
        System.out.println("Can't read document with id " + clientID);
    }
```

```
    // fetch XML data as a string and print the results
else {
    stringDoc = rs.getString(1);
    System.out.println(stringDoc);
}
. . .
  conn.close();
}
    catch (Exception e) { . . . }
}
```

This program prints a single row of data containing all the XML contact information for the specified customer.

Although not shown here, it's also possible to use XQuery to retrieve one or more entire XML documents, provided you don't need to incorporate parameter markers in your XQuery. Later in this chapter, you'll see a Java excerpt that uses XQuery to retrieve XML data.

6.5.2 Retrieve portions of XML documents

A common programming task involves retrieving portions of XML documents. The Java code in this example (Example 6-8) retrieves the names and primary e-mail addresses of customers with a status of "Silver." Customer name and status information are stored in SQL VARCHAR columns, while e-mail addresses are contained in XML documents in the "contactinfo" column.

In the interest of brevity, I've omitted code previously shown, including only those lines that are new or different.

Example 6-8   Retrieving relational data and XML fragments with SQL/XML

```
. . .
String status = "Silver";

try{
    // get a database connection
    . . . .
    // define, prepare, and execute a query that includes
    // (1) a path expression that will return an XML element and
    // (2) a parameter marker for a relational column value
    String query = "SELECT name, xmlquery('$c/Client/email[1]' " +
        " passing contactinfo as \"c\") " +
        " from clients where status = ?";
```

```
PreparedStatement selectStmt = conn.prepareStatement(query);
selectStmt.setString(1, status);
ResultSet rs = selectStmt.executeQuery();

// iterate over and print the results
while(rs.next() ){
    System.out.println("Name: " + rs.getString(1) +
        "   Email:  " + rs.getString(2));
}
. . .
// release resources
}
catch (Exception e) { . . . }
```

This code issues a SQL/XML statement that calls the XMLQuery function. It supplies a path expression to this function that causes DB2 to navigate to the first "email" element beneath the root "Client" element of the target XML documents. (Note that the path expression is case-sensitive.) The $c variable and the SQL FROM clause indicate where these target documents can be found: in the "contactinfo" column of the "clients" table. The SQL WHERE clause further restricts the target XML documents to those found only in rows in which the client's "status" is of a certain value ("Silver," in this method).

Output from this program may appear similar to Example 6-9.

Example 6-9   Sample output from previous application

```
Name: Lisa Hansen    Email:

Name: Amy Liu    Email:   <email>sailer555@yahoo.com</email>
. . . .
```

In this sample output, no e-mail information was returned for a qualifying customer (Lisa Hansen) because this element didn't exist in her XML "contactinfo" document.

6.5.3 Filtering on relational and XML predicates

Java programs can also instruct DB2 to filter query output based on conditions that apply to both XML and non-XML data. The following example builds on the previous one, returning the names and primary e-mail addresses of "Silver" customers who live in San Jose, California. This single query is projecting data from XML and non-XML columns as well as restricting data based on the contents of both XML and non-XML columns.

The excerpt below (Example 6-10) includes only portions of code that have changed from the previous example. In this case, the SELECT statement now invokes XMLExists as part of the WHERE clause to restrict results to customers who live in the specified city and state (defined in the city and state variables, respectively).

Example 6-10   Filtering XML data based on XML element values

```
. . .
String status = "Silver";
String state = "CA";
String city = "San Jose";
. . .
try{
    . . . .
    String query = "SELECT name, xmlquery('$c/Client/email[1]' " +
        " passing contactinfo as \"c\") " +
        " from clients where status = ?" +
        " and xmlexists('$c/Client/Address[state=$state][city=$city]' " +
        " passing contactinfo as \"c\", " +
        " cast(? as char(2)) as \"state\", " +
        " cast(? as varchar(30)) as \"city\" )";
    PreparedStatement selectStmt = conn.prepareStatement(query);
    selectStmt.setString(1, status);
    selectStmt.setString(2, state);
    selectStmt.setString(3, city);
    . . .
}
```

Most of the query should be familiar to you, so this section just concentrates on its final four lines. The XMLExists function instructs DB2 to determine if a given XML document contains a client address that includes a specific city and state. The PASSING clause specifies where XML documents can be found: in the "contactinfo" column. The CAST function is called twice to cast the values of the input parameters (for city and state) to appropriate data types.

The output from this program is similar to the output shown in Example 6-9, assuming both Lisa Hansen and Amy Liu live in San Jose, California.

6.5.4 Use XQuery as a top-level language

Although DB2 fully supports XQuery as a top-level language, the initial XQuery specification didn't address parameter markers. As a practical matter, this restricts the use of XQueries in Java applications. Previous sections illustrated how you can embed XQueries in SQL (using the XMLQuery and XMLExists functions, for example) to incorporate parameter markers. This section explores what you can do with pure XQuery in your Java applications.

Example 6-11 contains an XQuery similar to one presented in Chapter 5, "Querying XML data with XQuery" on page 63. This XQuery determines which customers live in San Jose, California. For each such customer, it constructs an XML fragment containing an "emailList" that includes all the e-mail addresses for that customer. Finally, it returns a sequence of emailLists.

Example 6-11   Retrieving XML fragments with XQuery

```
try{
    // get a database connection
    Connection conn = Conn.getConn();

    // define, prepare, and execute an XQuery (without SQL).
    // note that we must hard-code query predicate values.
    String query = "xquery for $y in db2-fn:xmlcolumn" +
        "('CLIENTS.CONTACTINFO')/Client " +
        "where $y/Address/city=\"San Jose\" and $y/Address/state=\"CA\"   " +
        "return <emailList> { $y/email } </emailList>";
    PreparedStatement selectStmt = conn.prepareStatement(query);
    ResultSet rs = selectStmt.executeQuery();

    // iterate over all items in the sequence and print results.
    while(rs.next() ){
        System.out.println(rs.getString(1));
    }

    // release all resources
    . . .
    // catch and handle any exceptions
    . . .
}
```

Two aspects of this query are worth noting. First, the query string begins with the keyword **xquery**. This instructs DB2 to use its XQuery parser to process the query. You need to do this whenever you use XQuery as the outermost language. Second, the query refers to the table and column names in upper case. XQuery is a case-sensitive language. Since DB2 typically folds table and column names into upper case when writing this information to its internal catalogs, the XQuery must match this information.

Sample output from this program is shown in Example 6-12. Because one "emailList" item is returned per qualifying customer, a quick scan of this output indicates that four customers qualified. The first qualifying record contains one e-mail address. The second contains none (perhaps because the customer didn't supply this information); as a result, its emailList is empty. The third qualifying record indicates that there are two e-mail addresses on record for this customer. The fourth contains one e-mail address for the customer.

Example 6-12   Sample output from previous application

```
<emailList><email>newemail@someplace.com</email></emailList>

<emailList/>

<emailList><email>beatlesfan36@hotmail.com</email>
<email>lennonfan36@hotmail.com</email></emailList>

<emailList><email>sailer555@yahoo.com</email></emailList>
```

You may wonder why the names of each qualifying customer were not included in our results. The answer is simple: XQuery works with XML data, and the customer names are stored in a SQL VARCHAR column. So, if you want the output to include the names of qualifying customers as well as their e-mail addresses, you would have to write a query that includes both SQL and XQuery.

6.6 Update and delete XML data

To update and delete XML data stored in DB2, you use SQL UPDATE and DELETE statements. These statements can include SQL/XML functions that restrict the target rows and columns based on XML element values stored within XML columns. For example, you can delete rows containing information about customers who live in a specific zip code or update XML (and non-XML data) only for customers who live in a given state.

Because the syntax for using SQL/XML functions in UPDATE and DELETE statements is the same syntax for using them in SELECT statements, the full code samples won't be repeated here. Instead, just brief excerpts are included. Let's consider the DELETE operations first.

6.6.1 Delete examples

Deleting a row that contains XML data is simple. Just use the SQL DELETE statement with a WHERE clause (if desired) to restrict the rows to be deleted. For example, the following code in Example 6-13 deletes the row for client ID 1885.

Example 6-13   Deleting data based on a relational data value

```
 . . .
  int clientID = 1885;
String query = "delete FROM clients WHERE id = ?";
  . . .
PreparedStatement stmt = conn.prepareStatement(query);
stmt.setInt(1, clientID);
if (stmt.executeUpdate() == 0) {
   System.out.println("No records deleted.");
}
else { System.out.println("Record(s) deleted."); }
  . . .
```

If you want to restrict your DELETE operations based on XML element values, simply invoke the appropriate SQL/XML functions in your WHERE clause. Example 6-14 uses the XMLExists function to specify that information about all clients who live in Maine (abbreviated "ME") should be deleted.

Example 6-14   Deleting data based on an XML element value

```
String state = "ME";
String query = "delete from clients " +
" where xmlexists('$y/Client/Address[state=$state]' " +
" passing clients.contactinfo as \"y\", " +
" cast(? as char(2)) as \"state\" )";
 . . .
PreparedStatement stmt = conn.prepareStatement(query);
stmt.setString(1, state);
 . . .
```

6.6.2 Update examples

You can update data in an XML column using the SQL UPDATE statement or a stored procedure, such as DB2XMLFUNCTIONS.XMLUPDATE. In both cases, updates to the XML column occur at a document level rather than an element level. However, programmers who update using the stored procedure don't need to supply the full XML document to DB2. They only need to specify the XML elements to be updated, and DB2 preserves the unchanged document data as well as updates the specified elements. Programmers issuing UPDATE statements need to specify the full document (not just the elements they want to change).

An article, "XML application migration from DB2 8.x to DB2 Viper, Part 1: Partial updates to XML documents in DB2 Viper", by Hardeep Singh in IBM

DeveloperWorks, May 11, 2006, discusses the XMLUPDATE stored procedure and provides you with sample code.

```
http://www-128.ibm.com/developerworks/db2/library/techarticle/dm-0605si
ngh
```

We do not discuss the XMLUPDATE stored procedure here. Instead, this section reviews two code samples that issue UPDATE statements. You should find the logic of both examples familiar. One uses an XML file to update the "clients" table, while another uses a character string containing XML.

Example 6-15 updates the contact information for client ID 1333 by using XML data contained in a file. Note that the new XML data is validated against a registered schema as part of the update operation.

Example 6-15   Updating XML data from a file

```
int clientID = 1333;
String fn = "c:/XMLFiles/Client1333.xml";  // input file
String query = "update clients set contactinfo = " +
   "xmlvalidate(? according to xmlschema id user1.mysample) " +
   "where id = ?";
. . .
PreparedStatement stmt = conn.prepareStatement(query);
stmt.setInt(2, clientID);
File file = new File(fn);
stmt.setBinaryStream(1, new FileInputStream(file), (int)file.length());
. . .
```

Of course, you can also use an XML query predicate to specify the customer contact records that you want to update. Again, you need to use SQL/XML functions to do so. Imagine that a customer, Amy Wang, wants you to update her fax number but she doesn't remember her client ID. Instead, she supplies her home phone number to help you locate her information. The following code excerpt (Example 6-16) uses XMLExists to restrict updates only to the record containing Amy's home phone number. Note that Amy's full contact information is supplied as a Java string containing the revised XML document.

Example 6-16   Updating XML data with a character string

```
String homeph = "4081114444";
String xml =
   "<?xml version=\"1.0\"?>" +
   "<Client>" +
   "<Address> " +
      "<street>54 Moorpark Ave.</street>" +
      "<city>San Jose</city>" +
```

```
        "<state>CA</state>" +
        "<zip>95110</zip>" +
    "</Address>" +
    "<phone>" +
        "<work>4084630110</work>" +
        "<home>4081114444</home>" +
        "<cell>4082223333</cell>" +
    "</phone>" +
        "<fax>4087773111</fax>" +
    "<email>sailer555@yahoo.com</email>" +
    "</Client>";

String query = "update clients set contactinfo = ?" +
    "where xmlexists('$y/Client/phone[home=$homeph]' " +
    " passing clients.contactinfo as \"y\", " +
    " cast(? as varchar(11)) as \"homeph\" )";
. . .
PreparedStatement stmt = conn.prepareStatement(query);
stmt.setString(1, xml);
stmt.setString(2, homeph);
. . .
```

6.7 Query builder

If you need help writing queries for your application, the Developer Workbench provides wizards that generate SQL/XML and XQueries. Because most Java programmers write applications that require parameter markers, they frequently use SQL/XML. This section steps through a brief example of how to use the SQL query builder to generate a SQL/XML statement similar to one included in Example 6-8 on page 93.

To generate an SQL/XML statement, perform the following steps:

1. Prepare your workspace.
2. Specify the characteristics of your query.
3. Execute your query.

Let's step through each of these in turn.

6.7.1 Prepare your workspace

SQL statements are created as part of a "Data project" accessible from the workbench's Data perspective. To create such a project, complete the following steps:

1. Open the Data perspective. Select **Window** → **Open Perspective** → **Other** → **Data**.

2. Create a connection to your target database. Right-mouse click inside the Database Explorer pane in the lower left corner. Select **New Connection** and specify your database name, user name, and password.

3. Create a new Data project. Right-mouse click inside the Data Project Explorer pane in the upper left corner. Select **New** → **Project** → **Data** → **Data Development Project**. When prompted, give the project a name of your choice, and associate it with the database connection you created previously.

With a database connection open and a Data project created, you're ready to build queries.

6.7.2 Build your query

To keep this tutorial simple, create a SQL/XML statement that returns the primary e-mail address of clients who have a certain status. The query will be similar to Example 6-17.

Example 6-17   Sample SQL/XML query

```
SELECT name, xmlquery('$c/Client/email[1]'
passing contactinfo as "c")
from clients where status = ?
```

Follow these steps to generate your query:

1. Launch the SQL Builder. Within your Data project, highlight the **SQL Scripts** folder and right-mouse click. Select **New** → **SQL Statement**. When prompted, accept the default for your project name and specify a name for your SQL statement. Accept the default for the statement type (SELECT) and elect to use the SQL builder. Click **Finish**.

2. Specify the table to be queried. Right-mouse click in the center pane and select **Add Table**. Expand your schema folder and select the "clients" table.

3. Specify the columns of interest. For this example, you need to include one column and the output of one function (XMLQuery) in the result set. To do so, complete the following steps:

   a. Check the "names" column displayed in the center pane.

b. Click the first row displayed in the Column tab beneath the center pane. Click the far right corner of this cell to display an arrow key and select **Build Expression**. Press **Enter**.

c. Select **Function** from the displayed menu.

d. Select **XML** as the function category and **XMLQuery** as the function. Next to Parameter Value 1, click the arrow in the **Value** cell and select **Edit Expression**.

e. Specify the appropriate path expression in the String Constant Builder: `$c/Client/email[1]`, and click **Finish** twice.

f. Alter the generated SQL statement to include a PASSING clause in the XQuery function. The final XQuery function should read: `'$c/Client/email[1]' passing contactinfo as "c"`

4. Specify the query predicate (WHERE clause). For this example, you need to add one query predicate for a relational column.

a. Under the Conditions tab beneath your SQL/XML statement, click the first row displayed in the Column tab. Click the arrow key in the far right of this cell and select the **status** column.

b. Click the **Operator** cell and select the equality ("**=**") operator.

c. Click the arrow key in the far right of the **Value** cell and select **Build Expression**. Press **Enter**.

d. Select **Constant** and then **String Constant** when prompted.

e. Specify a host variable name for user input (such as "status"). Click **Finish**.

6.7.3 Execute your query

After building your query, you're ready to run it.

1. Locate the query in your Data project, right-mouse click and select **Run SQL**.

2. When prompted, specify an input value for the customer status (such as "Gold" or "Silver"), and click **OK**.

3. Review the results in the Data Output pane.

6.8 Stored procedures

In networked environments, stored procedures often reduce the communication required between client applications and DB2. This, of course, improves runtime performance. With DB2 9, stored procedures may include XML parameters and variables.

While it's beyond the scope of this chapter to discuss stored procedure development in detail, a review is provided for one simple scenario so you can see how a DB2 stored procedure can be written to retrieve portions of XML documents. This scenario uses wizards in the Developer Workbench to generate, deploy, and run the necessary SQL stored procedure code. If desired, you can develop and deploy an equivalent SQL stored procedure using DB2's command line processor. In addition, you can write XML-based stored procedures in Java.

For this example, you will write a stored procedure that retrieves the names and primary e-mail addresses of clients with a certain status, just as you did earlier. Although this procedure is quite simple, it helps you understand how to generate SQL-based procedures that query and return XML data using built-in wizards.

To create this procedure, perform a few simple steps:

1. Prepare your workspace.
2. Specify the contents of your procedure.
3. Deploy and test your procedure.

Let's step through each of these in turn.

6.8.1 Prepare your workspace

Stored procedures are defined as part of a Data project. If you haven't already done so, open the Data perspective, establish a database connection, and create a Data project. For details, see 6.7.1, "Prepare your workspace" on page 101.

6.8.2 Create your procedure

Our SQL-based stored procedure invokes a single SQL/XML statement to query the "clients" table based on input from the caller. This procedure returns a single result set that contains a SQL VARCHAR column (for the client's name) and an XML column (for the client's e-mail). The query will be similar to Example 6-18.

Example 6-18 Sample SQL/XML query

```
SELECT name, xmlquery('$c/Client/email[1]'
passing contactinfo as "c")
from clients where status = ?
```

The process for building a SQL stored procedure that accesses XML data is no different from building a SQL procedure that accesses non-XML data. Here's one way to do so:

1. Define a new stored procedure. Expand your new Data project, highlight **Stored Procedures**, and right-mouse click. Select **New → Stored Procedure**. Follow the prompts to verify the project name and specify a stored procedure name. Keep the default language type as SQL.

2. Specify your SQL statements. When prompted, you can type your query statement directly or use the wizards to help you create one. The following steps are for the latter.

   a. Click **Create SQL**.

   b. Accept the defaults for the statement type (SELECT) and development process (guided through statement creation with wizards).

   c. Select the **clients** table as the target for your statement.

   d. Under the Columns tab, include two columns in the final result set. Select names, then select **Add → Function → Next**. In the following window, specify the function category as XML, and XMLQuery as the function signature. Click **Finish**.

   e. Under the Conditions tab, construct the SQL WHERE clause. Specify clients.status as the column, equals ("=") as the operator, and **:input** as the value.

   f. Modify the resulting SQL statement to include the appropriate path expression for retrieving the first e-mail address in the "contactinfo" column. Specifically, change the XMLQUERY line to read:
   `xmlquery('$c/Client/email[1]' passing contactinfo as "c")`

   g. Parse your query to verify there are no syntax errors.

3. Specify deployment information. In particular, you may find it helpful to Enable Debugging.

4. Optionally, review the generated SQL code. Click **Show SQL**. (See Figure 6-2 for a sample of what should appear.)

5. Complete the stored procedure. Click **Finish**.

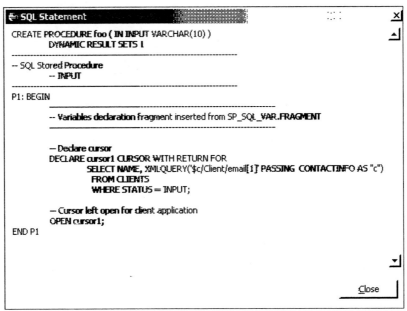

```
SQL Statement                                                    x

CREATE PROCEDURE foo ( IN INPUT VARCHAR(10) )
          DYNAMIC RESULT SETS 1
-----------------------------------------------------------------
-- SQL Stored Procedure
       -- INPUT
-----------------------------------------------------------------
P1: BEGIN
          -----------------------------------------------------------
          -- Variables declaration fragment inserted from SP_SQL_VAR.FRAGMENT
          -----------------------------------------------------------

          -- Declare cursor
          DECLARE cursor1 CURSOR WITH RETURN FOR
                  SELECT NAME, XMLQUERY('$c/Client/email[1]' PASSING CONTACTINFO AS "c")
                  FROM CLIENTS
                  WHERE STATUS = INPUT;

          -- Cursor left open for client application
          OPEN cursor1;
     END P1

                                                              Close
```

Figure 6-2   Sample code generated for SQL stored procedure involving XML data

6.8.3 Deploy and test your procedure

With your procedure created, you're now ready to deploy and test it. Follow these steps:

1. Deploy the procedure. Locate the procedure in your Data project, right-mouse click and select **Deploy**. Accept the defaults and click **Finish**. The Data Output pane in the lower right corner should note that your procedure has been successfully deployed.

2. Run the procedure. Locate the procedure in your Data project, right-mouse click, and select **Run**. When prompted, specify an input value for the customer status (such as "Gold" or "Silver"). Click **OK**, and view the results of your stored procedure in the Data Output pane.

You can call the stored procedure outside the Developer Workbench, if desired. For example, if you had named your procedure "getInfo," you could invoke the DB2 command line processor, connect to the database, and issue this statement shown in Example 6-19.

Example 6-19   Invoking your stored procedure

```
call getInfo('Silver')
```

6.9 Summary

Writing Java applications that work with DB2 XML data involves using familiar JDBC code to execute queries and process their results. IBM provides an Eclipse-based Developer Workbench with DB2 to help you code, test, and debug your work. Included in this workbench are wizards for exploring the contents of your databases, writing stored procedures that access XML and non-XML data, writing XQueries that access XML data, and writing SQL/XML statements that access XML and non-XML data.

7

Case study: Storebrand

With roots dating back to 1767 and fiscal year 2004 profits of 2.4 billion NOK (358 million USD), Storebrand Group is Norway's oldest and one of its biggest financial services companies, and a leading player throughout Scandinavia. The company provides life insurance, pension products, commercial retail banking and asset management to many of Norway's largest companies as well as to private individuals, municipalities, and public sector entities.[1]

► **Business need**: Improve business agility, ability to make timely and informed business decisions, and provide better customer service

► **Solution**: Implement a service-oriented architecture based on IBM DB2® and IBM WebSphere® solutions, including IBM DB2 9 data server (formerly known as "Viper")

► **Benefits**: Expected ability to handle five times as many customers; reduced order processing time; faster time to market with new products and product combinations; improved customer service through 24x7 online access and ability to view all orders; richer ability to query stored customer and product

---

[1] Information in this chapter was originally published as *Storebrand improves agility by integrating business processes with IBM solution*, IBM White Paper, May 17, 2006.

http://www-306.ibm.com/software/success/cssdb.nsf/cs/HSAZ-6PW3MW?OpenDo
   cument&Site=software

© Copyright IBM Corp. 2006. All rights reserved.

data for business insight; dramatically reduced time, complexity and cost to conduct database queries; improved productivity for programmers

7.1 Case Study overview

"With pureXML support available in IBM DB2 9, it is far easier, faster and less expensive to run queries, share and retrieve data, and make document changes in response to new business requirements without impacting applications." – Thore Thomassen

"Our development time using DB2 9 database is a radical improvement over existing XML shred technology. We are now able to make schema changes in minutes rather than days and will be able to dramatically improve our customer response time." – Thore Thomassen

7.2 Why IBM?

Storebrand is a longtime IBM customer and has worked with IBM in the testing and development of new products.

A well-recognized name in Norway, Storebrand rose to prominence due to its readiness and ability to meet the challenges of new situations. To maintain its reputation, ensure continued brisk growth, and improve its focus on customers in a highly competitive market, Storebrand sought to become a more agile business, one able to flexibly and quickly respond to customer needs. To achieve its goal, however, required overcoming significant hurdles: integrating its disparate products and IT infrastructures and then finding an optimal way to query its product and customer data.

Many of Storebrand's products and sub-products have their own IT solutions and associated business processes. Product and customer data is spread across numerous databases and a mix of mainframe, UNIX®, and Microsoft® Windows®-based platforms. Storebrand wanted to link all its products and processes to simplify and expedite orders, increase product customization, create product packages, speed time to market for new products and improve quality control, all while driving down costs. More recently, the company has sought a way to efficiently store and query transaction data to improve its ability to respond to customer requests and to make timely and informed business decisions.

7.3 Creating a single view of business-critical data

To create a unified and responsive information architecture for handling orders of financial products, Storebrand developed a service-oriented architecture (SOA)

— applications and information that can be broken apart as components and reused via a Web-services interface to create new business processes. IBM Global Services helped Storebrand implement its SOA using IBM DB2 Universal Database, IBM WebSphere Application Server, and IBM WebSphere MQ on IBM System z and IBM System i servers.

Storebrand has transformed tailor-made transactions to more efficient, standardized transactions through its SOA. A business services gateway based on Web services handles incoming transactions and provides Storebrand's legacy applications with reusable business services. Storebrand's integration architecture offers distributed transactions while also providing consistency and synchronization among legacy system applications.

7.4 IBM DB2 9 pureXML support enhances SOA

As a flexible way of exchanging data among devices, systems, and applications, XML and the ability to store it are key to Storebrand. All its product offerings are stored as XML documents known as a collection of large objects (CLOBs). While CLOBs enable more data to be stored in a database, they are difficult to retrieve and update. The next evolution of the company's SOA will include IBM DB2 9 database, which is the industry's first hybrid database management system (DBMS) that supports pure XML — that is, XML documents in their original structure — in addition to SQL and tabular data structures. DB2 9 provides performance improvements and greater flexibility for storing, searching, and managing XML. Storebrand is testing DB2 9 and plans to deploy it to store transaction records and business services.

By simplifying and speeding up queries and reporting capability, DB2 9 will enhance Storebrand's ability to make informed business decisions about its product offerings, while simultaneously reducing IT resource costs. "With the pure XML support available in IBM DB2 9, it is far easier, faster, and less expensive to run queries, share and retrieve data, and make document changes in response to new business requirements without impacting applications," explains Thore Thomassen, senior enterprise architect for Storebrand Group.

The ability to query data rapidly will also improve Storebrand's responsiveness to customers. "Until IBM DB2 9, it was impossible to comprehensively query product and customer data because of the way the information had to be stored," says Thomassen. "With DB2 9, we can, for example, easily and quickly respond to a corporate customer's request for order and status information on products purchased by one of its subsidiaries."

7.5 Improved quality and speed of offerings enhance customer service

With its SOA, Storebrand can more flexibly handle orders. It can provide customers with around-the-clock access to account information, accept orders 24x7 online, and control transaction flow to legacy systems to avoid performance bottlenecks. Storebrand has been able to shrink order processing time for many products. For example, an application for a license to implement a pension plan previously took up to three weeks to process but can now be completed in 10 minutes. Faster processing gives Storebrand the ability to handle five times the number of customer orders. Much of the manual data re-entry done by individual departments has also been eliminated, leading to fewer mistakes, higher quality, and more efficient customer service.

Storebrand can also rapidly introduce new products and product combinations simply by gluing together existing XML-based product definitions that it has for each of its products and sub-products. "This ability speeds our time to market, which is extremely important because customers will go elsewhere if they can't find the products they want," says Thomassen. The XML format also allows for variations in data, helping Storebrand to easily add new sub-products to a package without changing or slowing the transaction.

7.6 DB2 9 improves business agility

Storebrand conducted multiple tests using DB2 9 and found that it was able to perform queries, program searches, and make changes to pure XML data far more quickly and easily, while also improving programmers' productivity. The alternatives tested involved querying XML stored as CLOBs and shredding XML, which involves decomposing the data into multiple columns and sometimes tables to query it. These options have performance, cost, and manageability limitations.

Using DB2 9, queries that once took up to 36 hours shrunk to 10 minutes or less. Programming search processes required 30 minutes for pure XML data versus two to eight hours with the alternatives. The time it took programmers to prepare for a search shortened from one week to one half day. Updating XML schema in response to a business change was also much faster — five minutes compared to one week with shredding. Storebrand also achieved a 65 percent reduction in the amount of I/O code by converting 20 of its services to pure XML. "Our development time using DB2 9 database as our pure XML store is a radical improvement over existing XML shred technology. We are now able to make schema changes in minutes rather than days and will be able to dramatically improve our customer response time," says Thomassen. "In combination with our service-oriented architecture, DB2 9 can help us achieve, with far greater ease, our goal of using information on demand to readily respond to market changes and customer demand."

7.7 Key Components

Software:

- ▶ IBM DB2 9 (formerly codenamed "Viper")
- ▶ IBM DB2 Universal Database™
- ▶ IBM WebSphere Application Server
- ▶ IBM WebSphere MQ

Servers:

- ▶ IBM System i™
- ▶ IBM System z™

Services:

- ▶ IBM Global Services

For more information, please contact your IBM sales representative or IBM Business Partner.

Visit our Web site at:

`http://www.ibm.com/db2`

`http://www.ibm.com/websphere`

For more information on Storebrand, visit:

`http://www.storebrand.no`

Products and Services Used:

IBM products and services that were used in this case study:

- ▶ Hardware: iSeries Servers and zSeries Servers
- ▶ Software: DB2 Universal Database, WebSphere Application Server, and WebSphere MQ
- ▶ Operating System: UNIX
- ▶ Services: IBM Global Services

Related publications

The Web sites and publications listed in this section are considered particularly suitable for a more detailed discussion of the topics covered in this redbook.

Online resources

These Web sites and URLs are also relevant as further information sources:

► Information and resources for DB2 9 on Linux, UNIX, and Windows:

  http://www.ibm.com/db2/viper

► Information and resources for pureXML support in DB2 9:

  http://www.ibm.com/db2/xml

► IBM Systems Journal issue entitled "Celebrating 10 Years of XML":

  http://www.research.ibm.com/journal/sj45-2.html

How to get IBM Redbooks

You can search for, view, or download Redbooks, Redpapers, Hints and Tips, draft publications and Additional materials, as well as order hardcopy Redbooks or CD-ROMs, at this Web site:

  ibm.com/redbooks

Help from IBM

IBM Support and downloads

  ibm.com/support

IBM Global Services

  ibm.com/services

© Copyright IBM Corp. 2006. All rights reserved.

Index

Symbols
.NET environment 11
"native" support for XML 9

A
application heap size 40
application programming interfaces (APIs) 9

B
bilingual 10
binary large objects 4
BLOBs 4

C
C 11
call-level interface 11
CLOBs 4
COBOL 11
Control Center 67
Curly brackets 75

D
data type definitions (DTDs) 8
database management systems (DBMS) 4
DB2 Command Editor 67
DB2 Snapshot 11
DB2.NET 11
de-normalizing 6
Developer's Workbench 24
developerWorks 12
document decomposition technology 5

E
Eclipse 24
electronic data interchange (EDI) 3
enterprise application integration (EAI) 2
enterprise information integration (EII) 2
Exegenix 36
EXPLAIN 11
Extensible Markup Language (XML) 16

F
first-class data type 9
Full text search 10

H
hybrid DBMS 7

I
IMPORT 10
indexes 10
INSERT 10

J
Java (JDBC) 11
joins 6

M
MDXSYS Limited 37
multi-structured database management system 15
multi-structured database management system (DBMS) 15

N
namespaces 40
native support 9
normalized 6

P
parent/child relationships 5
persisting x, 4, 120
PHP 11

Q
query optimization 24

R
Redbooks Web site 113
    Contact us xii
RUNSTATS 11

© Copyright IBM Corp. 2006. All rights reserved.